For Terri, Nicole, and all the many survivors who shared their stories and their longing for God with me. I will be forever humbled by your trust and your courage.

"O God, you are my God,
earnestly I seek you;
my soul thirsts for you,
my body longs for you,
in a dry and weary land
where there is no water." (Psa 63:1)

Table of Contents

Acknowledgements

It would have been impossible to undergo the ten-year journey of writing this book without the support and encouragement of many people along the way. I am incredibly grateful to all of them, both named and unnamed, for the many ways in which they contributed to the making of this book.

I owe the foundations of my insatiable hunger to write to my mother, Patsy Greene Tiffany, who read to me constantly before I could read myself, recited poetry at the drop of a hat for almost any circumstance, drove me to the library weekly to feed my love of books, and read my awkward first attempts at writing short stories in grade school. I miss her every day, and I know that she would be so proud that I have accomplished what she always knew I could.

I am grateful to all the teachers, pastors, and colleagues who unlocked the secrets of the human mind and spirit for me and to the hundreds of clients over fourteen years who entrusted their stories to me and taught me about courage and the will to heal and thrive. I also owe much to the Academy for Spiritual Formation, a two-year program of The Upper Room, for grounding me in the theology that undergirds this book and for expanding my own ideas about the nature and image of God.

I have been fortunate to know a number of writers over the years who were gracious enough to allow me to pick their brains about the workings of the publishing world. Among them are Cathy Warner, Linda Douty, Suzanne Seaton, Kara Lassen Oliver, and Mary Huycke. It was Cathy Warner who recommended I submit my book to Wipf and Stock, and to her I am eternally grateful. She was also one of my biggest cheerleaders along the way.

I am also blessed with so many friends who have been my encouragers from day one. My deep gratitude goes out to Chris Packard, Ginny Miller, Juli Reinholz, Denise McGuiness, Roberta Egli, J.T. Greenleaf, Cathy

Warner (again), and Debra Dickerson. In addition, I give my spiritual director, Suzanne Seaton, credit for keeping me together when the going got rough and holding me accountable to my commitment to making this book a reality.

Many thanks to the women who were my readers, giving me invaluable advice on the many different aspects of this book: Jane Wray, who wields a wicked red pen, and whose advice on the finer points of grammar, punctuation, and style was greatly appreciated; and Chris Packard, Denise McGuiness, and Heather Rodenborg, who read for content and made this a better book.

Last, but not least, I must thank my family. To my adult children, Megan and Brian, and their spouses, Shauna and Kelly, thanks for being my cheering section. Your absolute faith in me and your desire to see me succeed has kept me going when times got rough. And to my husband, Tom, eternal thanks for putting up with me, for tolerating my mental absences when I was "in the zone," and for always believing in me. Your support has been my foundation. Love you to the moon and back!

Introduction

Survivors of child sexual abuse are victims of a silent holocaust, a holocaust of the soul. Unfortunately, the spiritual wounding of sexual abuse is often overlooked in discussions about the impact it has on the lives of survivors. Many books have been written to address the horror of sexual abuse for its victims, some of which offer help within a religious context and give tools to those who wish to use their faith as a resource for healing. Fewer address the issues of those whose faith is a stumbling block rather than a resource. While some survivors have experienced God and church as their refuge from the abuse,[1] others experience God as one who has rejected and abandoned them. This may render them unable to trust in the religious principles by which they were taught or the people or institutions who taught them. For these survivors, their spiritual struggles and questions must be addressed before they can find a positive spirituality that leads to hope and wholeness. That is the purpose of this book.

The material presented in these pages arises from my fourteen years as a mental health professional, primarily as a pastoral counselor, and five years as a spiritual director. I have had numerous clients who were survivors of child sexual abuse, and many of their stories appear in this book. I am indebted to them for their willingness to share their struggles and for their incredible courage in choosing to face their abuse head-on and travel the difficult journey toward healing.

I will be addressing several difficult issues in these pages: the nature of God, heaven and hell, forgiveness, and how one reconciles a loving God with the reality of a suffering world. These are questions with which humanity has wrestled for thousands of years, and the best theological minds have attempted to answer them for centuries with only a modicum of success. I do not have a degree in theology; however, it is said that anyone who

---

1. Guenther, *Holy Listening,* 133.

attempts to discover the nature of God is a theologian. That means that you, the reader, and I are all theologians. The answers I have come to after many years of walking with people through the darkest times of their lives are the only truth I have to offer. I hope that most readers will find in these pages a new way of perceiving God, believing God, and receiving the love and grace I believe God gives freely to all God's children.

It is important to note here that while I write from a primarily Judeo-Christian perspective, I do believe there are many paths to the one Divine Being. It is not my intent to exclude any reader who identifies with another of the world's major religions. An attempt has been made to include examples from Buddhism, Judaism, Islam, and Hinduism where applicable.

As a side note, I have chosen not to use gender-specific pronouns to refer to God. While this may result in awkward phrasing at times, I feel it important to be sensitive to survivors of abuse who struggle with the concept of a male God. Feminine pronouns may prove difficult for those from more traditional denominations, so I made the decision to eliminate pronouns altogether. The only exception will be when I am referring to Jesus.

A word of warning to those survivors of sexual abuse who open this book—it will not be easy to read. It contains real stories about real people. All their names have been changed, and some characters are actually composites of several survivors, but the events are representations of things that happen daily all over the world. The material may trigger memories and emotions thought long buried. In any process of healing, there is a period of upheaval as old beliefs and perceptions are questioned, and nothing seems certain anymore. This is actually a sign that growth and progress are just around the corner, but it is painful to go through nonetheless, particularly without support. Being in therapy or spiritual direction is highly recommended. Having someone who knows you well and can offer a healthy objectivity will be helpful as you explore the issues that may come up as you read. Read slowly, taking time to process the thoughts and feelings that are stirred by the material. Pay attention to how you are doing, and take a break if you need to. If you find yourself resistant to any of the healing practices offered throughout the book, process that with your therapist or spiritual director to see if it is merely resistance to facing something difficult or if you are truly not ready to go there yet. Not every exercise will be helpful for every reader.

It is hoped that therapists and spiritual directors will be some of the readers who delve into these pages. Perhaps this book will impress upon therapists the importance of addressing spiritual issues with their clients who have been victims of abuse. Too often this is an area that is ignored or avoided. There is so much fear that talking about spiritual things will step on someone's toes or violate professional codes of ethics. Many therapists have had virtually no training in this area and feel very uncomfortable talking about matters of faith. However, there has been in recent years a growing trend toward more holistic therapies that acknowledge the spiritual life of the client. There are many workshops and seminars available for those who are interested in learning how to address religious issues competently and with caring sensitivity. For those who still feel uncomfortable with this topic, referral to a spiritual director to aid the client in addressing the spiritual aspect of their healing is recommended.

Spiritual direction is an ancient practice of companioning. A spiritual director is someone who has been trained and feels called to journey with those who are on a spiritual path. They help their directees to see the ways in which the Divine is working in their lives, to find more healthy images of God, and incorporate meaningful spiritual practices into daily life. In the case of sexual abuse, they can also help survivors work through the distorted and damaging beliefs that interfere with healing and move toward a more loving relationship with the Divine.

For spiritual directors, awareness of the importance of addressing abuse issues in the spiritual direction session is essential. A directee's sexual violation should be neither avoided nor minimized. Certainly, there may be some discomfort about discussing such a painful subject. Society as a whole displays a remarkable avoidance in this area. People don't want to think about child sexual abuse. They don't want to acknowledge that abuse is happening under a cloak of secrecy in homes, schools, and churches all over America. They don't want to believe that their own children are at grave risk of such insidious violation. So it is understandable that spiritual directors may be somewhat reluctant to enter into such overwhelming territory. The other difficulty for the spiritual director is often a lack of knowledge about the impact of sexual abuse and what the director can do to help and not to harm. Certainly, the psychological implications can leave one feeling in over one's head. If a directee is not currently in therapy, they should be referred to a trusted, competent, and sensitive counselor or psychologist. A team of professionals that together address all aspects of a holistic approach is optimal. Even then, education about sexual abuse is vital. This book may be a start, but it is not enough. Many books on spiritual direction have

chapters devoted to this issue and can be invaluable in helping professionals walk with those who have been victimized. A list of these can be found
at the back of this book.

Hopefully, the families, spouses, and friends of survivors will also
find this book helpful as they seek to understand what their loved ones are
going through. Perhaps these words will make sense in a way that the victim's halting attempts to explain their spiritual struggles have not. Perhaps
they will learn ways to accept, encourage, and support the survivor in their
search for a healthier, more vital faith. Perhaps it will even propel them into
a closer examination of their own beliefs, resulting in a deeper, more fulfill-
ing relationship with God and with the survivor whose experience caused
them to read this book.

Each chapter of this book represents the significant issues my clients
have raised throughout many years of working with them in therapy or
spiritual direction. In chapter 1, I present a broad overview of the long-
term effects of sexual abuse on all aspects of the survivor's life. Chapter 2
addresses the belief by many victims that God hates them and allowed or
actively willed their abuse. Developmental deficits that interfere with faith
development are explored in chapter 3, and other roadblocks to faith are
discussed in chapter 4. A victim's conviction about being sent to hell for the
abuse and its aftermath is presented in chapters 5 and 6. Closely connected
are the survivor's doubts about the perpetrator's eternal punishment, which
are addressed in chapter 7. Chapter 8 includes a deeper look at survivors'
images of God and some possible healing alternatives. Chapter 9 explores
the why of human suffering, and finally, chapter 10 offers hope for transformation and meaning in the context of the suffering of child sexual abuse.

All these issues are addressed through a combination of story, Scripture, theological discourse, psychological knowledge, and spiritual guidance. Embedded within each chapter are some suggested exercises that may
be helpful in the healing process. Again, I encourage the reader to listen to
their inner voice about his or her readiness for a particular practice. Take
your time. Feel free to only do the practices that fit you and your needs. This
book is meant to support your journey, not be a rigid prescription of what
you should do to "get better." Healing comes from many sources, and this
book is only one.

1

"How Long, O Lord?"
Exploring the Long-Term Effects of Child Sexual Abuse

*"How long, O Lord? Will you forget me forever? How long will you hide your
face from me? How long must I wrestle with my thoughts and every day
have sorrow in my heart? How long will my enemy triumph over me?"*
—PSALM 13:1–2

Rough estimates are that one in three girls and one in seven boys will
experience at least one episode of molestation by the time they reach
age eighteen. One in ten of those will be the victims of ongoing sexual
abuse. Between 70 percent and 90 percent of all cases of sexual abuse are
perpetrated by family members, trusted friends, youth leaders, or caregivers. Sexual abuse occurs in an atmosphere of secrecy and shame, and the
majority of incidents are never reported. This means the real number of
victims can never be known, but they are all around us, and they have been
wounded in ways few people can imagine. Their abuse has impacted every
aspect of their lives.

While the intent of this book is to explore and address the *spiritual*
issues of the sexual abuse survivor, it is important to understand how all-
encompassing the effects of sexual abuse can be on the entire psyche of a
survivor, and how many areas of functioning can be impaired. The purpose
of this chapter is to help readers place the wound to a survivor's spirituality
within the context of the totality of their abuse's impact across their lifespan.

Before moving on, it is important to note that the effects of child sexual abuse on its survivors are not the same for everyone. Some survivors, despite their pain, are able to lead relatively healthy lives. For others, the impact of abuse is long-term and permeates every aspect of their lives. However, even among those who struggle, few will experience all of the following potential effects of abuse. It is hoped that readers will recognize what is true for them and what is not. And it is crucial that survivors not minimize their experience of abuse if it does not fit into every category of injury mentioned here.

Nonetheless, many survivors do experience daily reminders of what they have suffered, and it can feel as though their lives are defined by the abuse. They might wonder if a day will ever come when they do not think about what happened to them. They long for a time when their behavior is not dictated by fear, shame, anguish, and a deep need to protect themselves from further pain. Memories may pummel their minds at unexpected times and inappropriate places, and they are often unable to control these intrusive images and feelings. Even when the perpetrators are dead, in prison, or far removed from them by distance and/or lack of contact, survivors may still feel as though their abusers have triumphed by virtue of the ongoing effect of these memories on their everyday lives.

Other survivors may not even recognize that what happened to them was sexual abuse at all. Sometimes the gradual grooming of a victim and the blurring of boundaries cause the survivor to be unable to name the abuse for what it was. Some perpetrators are so subtle in their behaviors that it is difficult to know when they have crossed the line from inappropriate to abusive. Even something as noninvasive as forcing a child to disrobe, urinate, or bathe in front of the offender when the child is past the age of needing adult supervision can be considered abuse. A good guideline is whether the behavior made a victim feel uneasy or uncomfortable, causing him or her to develop an aversion to the perpetrator. Unfortunately for these survivors, without being able to label what they experienced as sexual abuse, they are all the more confused by the long-term effects of their victimization.

The areas of functioning that are affected by sexual abuse can include self-image, emotions, relationships, occupational functioning, health problems, sexuality, and spirituality. The severity of symptoms can be influenced by the duration and frequency of abuse, the age at onset of abuse, and the type of sexual activity. Use of force or violence, the relationship between victim and perpetrator, and the family's response to reported abuse are additional considerations. The overall atmosphere of a victim's childhood home may also impact how they respond to the abuse and how they think and feel about themselves and the abuse they suffered. Children raised by dominating parents will be all the more fearful to disclose and more likely to blame themselves, not being able to name the abuse for what it was.

As we explore these different areas, remember that there is no particular way a survivor *should* react to sexual abuse. These are merely many of the typical ways in which survivors may be affected.

HEALING PRACTICE 1

At times, the ways in which the abuse you suffered infiltrates and infects every area of your life can be overwhelming. Like Job in the Old Testament, it probably feels like you have lost everything—health, happiness, positive relationships, meaningful work, and the ability to be "normal." In the Bible, one of Job's friends seeks to reassure him in his suffering with these words: "(God) will yet fill your mouth with laughter and your lips with shouts of joy" (Job 8:21) He could foresee a time when Job's life would be restored, healing would come, and the sun would shine again.

One of the hardest things for abuse survivors to do is have hope. It is a very scary thing when all you have known is pain and loss. To hope and have those hopes dashed would be devastating. See if you can identify just one area of your life where a small ray of light is already shining, for example, a positive relationship, good health, or an activity that gives you enjoyment.

- Can you allow yourself to acknowledge this light and let it continue to be there? It is not necessary for you to believe it will grow or expand to other areas of your life. It can just be what it is right now.

- Allow yourself to experience the light. What does it feel like? What difference does this make in your daily life?

Impact on Self-Image

Almost universally, sexual abuse survivors have an extremely poor sense of self. Often, they learn to define themselves by the cues they receive within the context of the abusive relationship. They then spend so much energy learning to read the cues of the abuser—his facial expressions, his moods, his vocal and body cues, and any signs of arousal—that they become experts in the art of interpreting the body language and nonverbal communication of others.[1, 2] This was a survival strategy developed to anticipate the abuser's wants and needs in order to keep him happy and thus avoid or minimize abuse.[3] As a result, survivors are highly oriented to other people and to their external environment, which they scan constantly for potential danger. Conversely, they have little to no awareness of their own internal world. Many times, survivors will tell me that they don't really know who they are. They are afraid of expressing any kind of opinion or want, lest it cause displeasure or anger in another. This results in them not having opinions or preferences at all. These are people pleasers who try to go with the flow and always acquiesce to the wants and needs of others.

Survivors almost always view themselves with loathing and disgust. They may carry shame around with them as a constant burden and frequently verbalize a sense of their own worthlessness. It is virtually impossible for many of them to view themselves as worthwhile individuals with gifts, traits, and talents that others might value. This comes from an innate belief that the abuse happened because they were bad and deserving of punishment. Perpetrators often reinforce these beliefs with statements to that effect. We will discuss this more in future chapters.

Another area related to self-image is the way in which sexual abuse survivors view their bodies. Many of them felt betrayed by their bodies. It was their body that caused them their deepest pain, and they want nothing to do with it. Some survivors believe they somehow caused their bodies to respond to the abuse with arousal or physical desire and thus hate themselves and their bodies for behaving in what was a strictly instinctual response. In either case, a common aftereffect is for survivors to be completely cut off from any kind of body awareness. In some, this is so extreme that the body may exhibit symptoms of disease or injury long before the survivor actually notices them.[4] Many are overweight, as if to deter any sexual attention at all, and dress in large, loose clothing to cover up the

1. While it is true that both women and men can be perpetrators of child sexual abuse, the vast majority of abusers are men. Therefore, for simplicity's sake, I will hereafter use the male pronoun when referring to a victim's abuser except in specific cases where the abuser was indeed a woman.

2. Herman, *Trauma and Recovery*, 99.

3. Carnes, *The Betrayal Bond*, 125.

4. Courtois, *Incest Wound*, 106.

physical manifestations of their gender or sexuality. Excess weight and baggy clothing act as a buffer between them and the world. Other survivors may be quite thin. They diet to extremes, exercise to excess, or starve themselves in a seeming attempt to punish their bodies for what happened. Being too thin is another way of desexualizing the body by eliminating the curves that might attract someone's attention.

HEALING PRACTICE 2

The shame that survivors feel is pervasive and almost universal. This shame makes you feel separate from others and from God. It is hard to imagine that people would want to be with you or that God could possibly love you. Following is a poem by Hafiz, a Sufi mystic of the 14th century, which speaks to the loss others feel when your shame and guilt cause you to draw away from connection with them:

Stay With Us

You

Leave

Our company when you speak

Of Shame

And this makes

Everyone in the Tavern sad.

Stay with us

As we do the hardest work of rarely

Laying down

That pick and

Shovel

That will keep

Revealing our deeper kinship

With

God,

That will keep revealing
Our own divine
Worth.

You leave the company of the Beloved's friends
Whenever you speak of
Guilt,

And this makes
Everyone in the Tavern
Very sad.

Stay with us tonight
As we weave love

And reveal ourselves,
Reveal ourselves

As His Precious
Garments.[5]

- Can you imagine that others might be deeply saddened by the shame that keeps you from getting close to them? Who in your life might feel that way?

- If your shame were a garment, what would it look like? If you were to remove it and reveal the precious garment of the Beloved underneath, what might that look like? Imagine its colors, patterns, and texture. How would it feel?

- If you want, write in your journal about this experience.

Emotional Impact

The emotional lives of many sexual abuse survivors can be full of turmoil. Conflicting emotions, such as simultaneous love and hate or pain and

5. Ladinsky, *The Gift*, 284–85.

pleasure, can create a chaotic inner world that is confusing and uncomfortable.[6] Anxiety and fear may be their constant companions. They may have great difficulty falling asleep, and when they do, their sleep can be haunted by nightmares of the abuse. One night, Terri, a young professional in her late twenties, had a dream of her long-dead abuser that was so intense and real, she awoke with her pistol in her hand as if to protect herself from a man who wasn't there. Another client, Nicole, regularly sleeps with every light in her apartment ablaze in order to keep the darkness at bay. Sometimes, she even resorts to sleeping under her dining room table—anywhere but in her bed, a place of horrific memories and hideous nightmares.

Some survivors' fears may cause them to experience panic attacks and phobias that may be hard for others to understand. Nicole is terrified of candles due to being burned and tortured by an older teen with an obsession with the satanic. This makes the Christmas Eve tradition of lighting candles more difficult for her than her fellow parishioners can possibly imagine. Victims of abuse have often been restrained or confined during episodes of molestation or punishment, which leads to claustrophobia when they are adults. These are people who need to know where all the exits are, and make sure that they situate themselves where they can see everything that is going on, especially when they are in strange surroundings. Other phobias I have witnessed in my clients include uniforms, certain types of music, particular smells, and thunderstorms—virtually anything that might trigger a memory of abuse. Sheila was eight years old when her uncle began molesting her. One time, a storm broke out just as he was getting dressed. A sudden clap of thunder startled the young girl, and her abuser said, "God must really be angry at you. If you tell anyone what you did, he's going to get you." It took much therapy for her to view thunderstorms in a healthier way.

Another emotional artifact of abuse is depression. Most of the abuse survivors I have seen in my practice have needed to be on antidepressant medication, some for a period of a year or so, some indefinitely. This depression can be very deep. According to Christine Courtois, author of the seminal book *Healing the Incest Wound*, incest survivors are much more likely to exhibit suicidal thoughts and behaviors or to engage in acts of self-harm than the general population.[7] Some depressed survivors seem to use suicidal thoughts as a way of gaining control over the internal chaos they

6. Meyer, *Through the Fire*, 34.
7. Courtois, *Incest Wound*, 105.

are experiencing. When life feels out of control, they at least know there is one choice that is within their power to make. Sometimes the thought itself is enough to make them feel more calm and in control. For others, self-mutilation is the means by which they exercise control. This is a pain that *they* can control, a pain that they have the power to stop or start, and it is a distraction from the emotional pain that haunts their days and nights.[8] By virtue of the power that was exerted over the survivor in immensely harmful ways, some feel a great sense of powerlessness or helplessness. Such was Nicole's sense of helplessness that when a would-be burglar rattled her front doorknob, she didn't even bother to call the police. The police had been called many times in the course of her childhood but had done nothing to stop her abuse, so she had become resigned to the fact that her purpose in life was for others to use, harm, or exploit her for their own ends. Calling the police seemed to her to be a pointless activity.

All victims of sexual abuse are defenseless against their perpetrators' will to abuse them. Sexual abuse is an act of power. When abusers aggress powerfully against their victims, it takes away any power that an innocent child might have had to determine the course of their own lives. Survivors have learned time after time that they are helpless, and this belief can carry over into adulthood. They may develop an external locus of control, a view of the world as a place in which things happen *to* them rather than one in which they have the power to effect change.

Emotional detachment or deadening may also be experienced. Many survivors learned very early on to suppress their painful feelings. Unfortunately, it is not possible to suppress selectively, so it is not only the painful emotions that get frozen, but also any fleeting happiness or enjoyment. Survivors are often aware of a seething cauldron of anger inside them, and they are terrified of what might happen if they dare to express even a little of this rage. They fear that if the anger were to be released they would lose all control and possibly become violent. They may associate anger with their abusers and do not want to be like them in any way. In addition, survivors often come from dysfunctional family systems where feelings get denied, minimized, or invalidated. They learn to shut down those emotions and allow others to dictate to them how they should feel. Their perpetrators compound matters when they punish expressions of fear or pain. Typically, tears are absolutely forbidden. By the time they get to adulthood, survivors may have great difficulty in allowing themselves to cry for fear of

---

8. Clark, with Henslin, *Cutter's Mind,* 175.

punishment or loss of control. They have not let themselves cry for so long, they think that if they begin, they will never be able to stop.

Interpersonal Impact

The primary issue in most abuse survivor's relationships is trust. Some survivors find it very difficult to trust, while others trust people indiscriminately. Sometimes the distrust is specific to the gender of their abusers, and sometimes not.[9] Those who have difficulty trusting are usually isolated, aloof, and emotionally cut off from people. They are very sensitive to slights and regularly test the commitment of their friends and loved ones, which can ultimately drive people who would be close away, bringing about a self-fulfilling prophecy. On the other hand, those who are too trusting can be readily manipulated or exploited, thus leaving the door open to re-victimization. Their naiveté and desire to please make them easy prey for those who would take advantage of them.

Many survivors have great difficulty with intimacy. The emotional deadening mentioned previously can function as a protective device that keeps others from getting too close to them. They maintain distance in part because of their fear of being hurt again and partially due to the anxiety that if people get to know them, they will discover the awful secret—that he or she is a horrible person, shameful, flawed, and unworthy of love. This fear of intimacy extends even to casual physical contact. Terri does not like anyone to hug her. Everyone on her staff knows this, but occasionally someone new will inadvertently give her a hug in greeting, and a collective gasp goes up from her co-workers as they wait to see how Terri will respond.

Other survivors enter into relationships quite compulsively and cling to the people in their lives ferociously. They have a deep fear of abandonment. Their learned helplessness makes them quite needy, and they often assume a victim role in their interactions with others in order to be taken care of. Another alternative is for them to take on a rescuer role, which allows them to be in control of the relationship. They believe that if they are needed enough, the other person won't leave them.

While much of what we have already discussed holds true in both social interactions and romantic partnerships, there are some issues that are specific to a survivor's intimate relationships. Sex abuse survivors often enter into committed relationships with great hesitancy, although the

9. Courtois, *Incest Wound*, 111.

opposite is also true. A greater proportion of survivors remain unmarried than the general population, but some of those who do marry do so in desperation.[10] Ginger is a 42-year-old physician's assistant who has been married four times. Each time a marriage ended, she was already in a relationship with another man. Being on her own was too frightening to contemplate, so whenever her marriages became troubled, she began unconsciously looking for the next "white knight" to rescue her from an intolerable situation. These marriages reflected the common patterns of other survivors—they were either abusive or neglectful, sometimes both, but almost always reflecting the dynamics of the survivor's family of origin. Partners may be either dominating—further victimizing the survivor—or weak and ineffectual, giving the survivor control of the relationship but meeting few of her needs.

Child sexual abuse can have a significant impact on the families of its victims. Even in the healthiest of families, abuse is difficult to respond to appropriately, but for families that were already dysfunctional, the dynamics of sexual abuse can create an even more toxic effect. Sometimes the abuser is a member of the dysfunctional family system, which usually brings with it greater levels of pain and suffering for the victim. Even when that is not the case, many parents have utterly failed to protect their child from the abuse he or she suffered. They ignored, denied, or minimized the abuse, and sometimes even blamed the victim for what was happening. Seldom do these dysfunctional families in which abuse has occurred exhibit healthy patterns of behavior. Instead, they are often verbally and/or physically abusive, rigid and controlling, and lacking in love and affection. As a result, many of the survivor's family relationships remain troubled into adulthood. Family members rarely support a survivor's efforts at healing and growth, often turning him or her into the family scapegoat.[11] The family mantra is often, "You just need to get over it!" When survivors have been raised with these painful family dynamics, they can have extreme difficulty detaching themselves from family ties or setting clear boundaries that protect them from further emotional wounding. Nicole and Terri both have families that are exploitative and manipulative, and despite years of therapy, they find themselves sucked back into the trap time and time again.

10. Ibid., 112.

11. Davis, *Allies in Healing*, 23.

Vocational Impact

The replication of unhealthy family dynamics often carries over into the workplace as well.[12] Jill, whose father often told graphically sexual jokes, worked with several colleagues whose sense of humor was equally raunchy. They continued in this vein despite Jill's obvious discomfort. Survivors frequently experience difficulties with their co-workers and supervisors, and are prone to being exploited and sometimes even abused. They seem to have particular difficulty with authority figures. Nicole is a teacher whose principal would regularly call her into her office and berate her for hours over minor deviations from policy. These abuses are rarely reported, since survivors are unaware that this is inappropriate and unacceptable.

A survivor's career path may be erratic at best. Post-traumatic stress symptoms have usually made it difficult for them to succeed in the classroom, making higher education challenging and, for some, impossible. Even when they do complete a degree program, their lack of identity and low self-esteem make choosing a vocation problematic. Major decisions do not come easily to them. Some survivors are unprepared for a "real world" environment and may have unrealistic ideas about what might be expected of them or what they are able to accomplish.

Trauma can also impact the survivor's ability to function well at job tasks that others perform without difficulty. The abuse disrupted normal developmental stages and tasks, leaving them floundering and incapable of keeping up with the demands of their job.[13] Conversely, there are some who have used achievement as a way of escaping their feelings about the abuse and about themselves.[14] Hard work is their means of controlling their lives, avoiding a social life, and receiving the affirmation they so desperately need. They are top performers, and their sense of well-being depends on it.

Physical Impact

Traumatic sexual abuse leaves a powerful physical mark on the bodies of its victims. Many survivors suffer intense flashbacks in which the body re-experiences trauma. They quite literally feel as if the abuser was performing sexual acts that occurred years before. In my office, with their perpetrator

12. Ibid., 24.

13. Courtois, *Incest Wound*, 114.

14. Davis, *Allies in Healing*, 24.

nowhere near, these survivors choke, grimace, writhe, jerk, and otherwise respond in the present to something that happened to them when they were helpless children. Alice, upon reliving an act of fellatio, was so nauseated by the taste in her mouth that I had to give her a piece of gum to relieve the sensation. This kind of experience often causes survivors to question their sanity, because they know what they are feeling is not real.

Nevertheless, there are plenty of other symptoms that are most definitely real. Survivors often experience chronic pain, especially of the genitals, as well as other genital, urinary, and gastrointestinal disorders.[15] Anxiety can lead to stress-related problems such as headaches, TMJ, insomnia, and high blood pressure. All these medical problems present a significant obstacle for patients with a history of abuse. Many survivors have a deep fear of doctors and medical procedures, particularly in the gynecological field. This is in part related to their shame as well as their reluctance to remove clothing or be touched in any way. Sometimes, a doctor's examination, while entirely appropriate in the medical context, replicates their abuse. Terri hated going to the dentist, because holding her mouth open for long periods of time reminded her of the oral sex forced upon her by her perpetrator. There is another issue at work here as well. At least three of my clients have experienced abuse at the hands of doctors, and another was forced to participate in a role-play scenario in which her perpetrator was dressed as a doctor.

Addiction to alcohol and other substances is another common concern. Substances are used to numb a survivor's psychic pain at great cost to their physical health. Even highly functioning survivors may rely on alcohol or drugs at the end of a workday to relax, so great is the energy required to maintain the illusion of someone who has it all together. Sometimes, addictive substances were given to victims by their perpetrators. Offenders often use alcohol to "loosen up" their potential victims. Joe, a young man whose grandfather anally raped him for years, suffers from a cocaine addiction. Although he hasn't used for quite some time, he often experiences flashbacks of the many times his abuser gave him cocaine in order to enhance his sexual response. When life starts to feel out of control, it takes everything Joe has to fight his powerful cravings for cocaine.

---

15. Courtois, *Incest Wound*, 106.

Sexual Impact

It should come as no surprise that the sexual functioning of the vast majority of abuse survivors is especially troubled. Sexual abuse disrupts normal psychosexual development and short-circuits the dating and courtship patterns of adolescents and young adults. They end up having no idea how to have a normal and healthy sexual relationship. Consequently, survivors gravitate to either of the two ends of the sexual spectrum—they are either promiscuous or asexual, sometimes vacillating between the two.[16] Bonnie, who suffered almost constant episodes of incest for over seventeen years, developed dissociative identity disorder (also known as multiple personality disorder) in order to cope with the enormity of her abuse. Her host personality, who had repressed all memory of the abuse, was a virgin. She went on her first date at the age of nineteen and had such a strong startle response when the boy tried to hold her hand that he never called her again. Nearly twenty years later, she still has not been on another date. Unbeknownst to her, one of her alter personalities spent her college years having sex with any young man who showed the slightest interest in her. She had learned what men wanted and thought sex was the only way to get their attention or affection.

For some women, their heightened sexuality leads them into prostitution. Many studies have determined that the percentage of prostitutes who have been sexually abused is quite high. Glenda Hope, a Presbyterian pastor who works with prostitutes in the Tenderloin district of San Francisco, claims that at least 70 percent of prostitutes endured long-term sexual abuse.[17] These women may feel that providing sex for money is all they're good for, the only thing they know how to do well. Unfortunately, prostitution puts them at grave risk for sexually transmitted diseases and criminal violence. Almost all of them turn to drugs in an attempt to forget about what they are doing to themselves. It is a soul-destroying life.

The sexualization of their bodies from a very young age has a profound effect even on the survivors who avoid any kind of sexual activity with another person. Some of the female survivors I know who are most afraid of intimate relationships masturbate on a frequent basis. For some, this is a self-soothing behavior that reduces anxiety and emotional upset. Others experience almost constant arousal from remembered abuse and

16. Ibid., 107
17. Hope, "Bearing Witness."

masturbate in order to get relief from their sexual feelings. Often, their flashbacks actually lead to spontaneous orgasms which can occur without any sexual touch at all. This is usually a source of great shame.

Survivors of sexual abuse are also often confused as to their sexual orientation. This is particularly true of boys who have been molested by a male perpetrator. Because they have had sexual relations with another male, they often wonder if that means they are homosexual. If they experienced arousal despite their aversion to what was happening, this complicates the issue even further. In female survivors, there is a significant percentage who might otherwise be heterosexual but who choose a lesbian lifestyle, just because they feel safer and less likely to be hurt by a woman.[18] It also helps them avoid the many gender-related visual triggers that could cause flashbacks.

Even when a survivor has been able to surmount their fear of intimate relationships and enter into a committed romantic partnership, their sex life is usually fraught with conflict. Survivors often try to avoid sex entirely. There are often arguments with their partner about frequency and the conditions under which they are willing to engage in sexual intimacy. Certain positions or sexual acts are to be avoided. There are rules about specific types of touch, levels of nudity, and the amount of light in the room. Brenda was molested by her older sister as a child, and oral sex was the primary activity that was forced upon her. Now married with three children, Brenda cannot tolerate oral sex, despite her husband's reasonable desire for this common sex act. She is able to be sexual with him in every other way but that. Sometimes sexual intimacy triggers flashbacks. When that happens, the partner must put their own feelings on hold and give comfort to the survivor who is emotionally distressed. In order to avoid this, some survivors learn to dissociate from the sex act, inducing a sort of "out-of-body" experience. This leaves their partner feeling as though they are making love to an automaton, and the marriage suffers from a lack of emotional intimacy.

Spiritual Impact

Margaret Scharf, a Dominican nun, writes, "The soul is the seat of emotion, intuition, and receptivity to God, as well as to others, deep within

18. Courtois, *Incest Wound*, 108–9.

us."[19] The experience of sexual abuse has a profound impact on the soul. For some people, the question of how a loving God can allow suffering in the world is merely a philosophical exercise. For abuse survivors who have endured horrible trauma, it is a question that is all too personal. They struggle daily with deep theological questions about a suffering humanity and the nature of God. Those survivors who were raised in the church often fall away from religion when they reach adulthood. According to one study, sexual abuse survivors are significantly more likely to describe themselves as "non-practitioners" of religion than those without an abuse history.[20] They feel alienated from God and from church members who seem to be the beneficiaries of God's blessings while survivors would be hard-pressed to name any blessings in their lives. Some feel quite uncomfortable inside a church building. Their shame makes them feel that they don't belong in this holy place. A friend of mine who experienced cult abuse as a child once told me there was a period of several years during which it took every ounce of his effort to walk through the door of a church. Unfortunately, he happened to be the pastor of that church at the time! Other survivors do attend church regularly but find no comfort or meaning in the rituals of worship. They go through the motions and maintain a façade of faithfulness, while keeping their distance from anything that might penetrate their carefully constructed defenses.

As mentioned previously, survivors have very little sense of self, which causes them to have difficulty in knowing or articulating what they believe. Low self-esteem undercuts their best efforts to find a meaningful faith. Terri expressed this very well in an e-mail once when I asked her what Christmas meant to her: "I have been thinking about what Christmas means to me, and I'm not really sure. I really don't know a lot about what I truly believe. I want to believe in the miracle of Christmas, but I often think I am not deserving, and it is hard to imagine a love that is unconditional. I pray to God every night, and I believe in Jesus, but it is scary."

Because of the rigidity often found in the survivor's family of origin, they rarely consider exploring other faiths or denominations in order to find a spirituality that is more loving, more accepting, and more healing. Mampta, a former client of East Indian descent, was raised in a controlling and highly overprotective household. Her father treated her like a fragile princess and isolated her from typical real-world experiences. During her

19. Scharf, "Stages of Faith."

20. Finkelhor et al., "Sexual abuse," 395.

many years of schooling, she was not allowed to drive or hold a job. If her father was challenged in any way, he would fly into frightening rages. He also crept into her room in the dark of night and molested her on a regular basis. This man held absolute sway over her. In my therapy work, I occasionally use a technique called sand tray in which clients choose from a wide variety of miniature objects and place them in a shallow tray of sand. This is a projective technique that elicits previously non-verbalized issues, memories, and emotions. At one point in Mampta's therapy, I asked her do a sand tray in my office. In one part of the tray, she placed a statuette of the Hindu god Shiva in front of a treasure chest holding a number of brightly colored stones. Mampta's explanation for this was that Shiva was blocking her from getting to the chest. As we explored this, she became aware that her father's Hindu faith, coupled with her fear of him, was preventing her from probing the riches of her own deep spirituality. She had rejected Hinduism, but was afraid to look beyond it to other ways of believing and expressing her faith. This insight freed her to become more aware of what was already inside her and to find a new path for living this spirituality in tangible and meaningful ways.

Mampta discovered what some other survivors also have, that when one has been deeply wounded in the context of their childhood religion, spiritual healing may not be possible in that same environment. This means that moving beyond the denomination or religion of one's childhood might be a possibility for the seeking person to consider. In general, there are many similarities and points of agreement among the teachings of the major religions of the world, and I believe there is much to value in most of them. There are many paths that lead to the one God.

While many survivors are agnostic, I have rarely met any who are atheists. When this does happen, it usually occurs among those who have not had any religious upbringing at all. Some would like to reject the idea of God but cannot. This often causes them great anguish, because they believe they fall so short of God's will that they will be absolutely rejected by God. Sometimes their images of the divine are more reflective of their abuser than of a loving God. For example, Carla was sexually abused throughout childhood by her older brother and some of his friends. While she was able to sustain her faith in God, she floundered when it came to the person of Jesus. In Christian doctrine, all men and women are the children of God, and if Jesus is the son of God, then in Carla's eyes that made him her brother as well. Since her earthly brother was abusive, she thought Jesus must be abusive, too. These and many other issues pertaining to the spiritual lives of survivors will be addressed in the following chapters.

HEALING PRACTICE 3

While many survivors of abuse do have a belief in God, however shaky that might be, what about those among you who do consider yourselves to be atheists? Consider this passage from *Earth and Altar*, by Eugene Peterson:

> The atheist is not always the enemy. Atheists can be among a Christian's best friends. Atheists, for instance, whose atheism develops out of protest: angry about what is wrong with the world, they are roused to passionate defiance. That a good God permits the birth of crippled children, that a loving God allows rape and torture, that a sovereign God stands aside while the murderous regime of a Genghis Khan or an Adolf Hitler runs its course—such outrageous paradoxes simply cannot be countenanced. So God is eliminated. The removal of God does not reduce the suffering, but it does wipe out the paradox. Such atheism is not the result of logical (or illogical) thought; it is sheer protest. Anger over the suffering and unfairness in the world becomes anger against the God who permits it. Defiance is expressed by denial. Such atheism is commonly full of compassion. It suffers and rages. It is deeply spiritual, in touch with the human condition and eternal values.[21]

Belief in God, then, is not a prerequisite for spirituality. Your spirituality may be a spirituality of nature, or of compassion for a suffering humanity, or of special moments with loved ones. You might find that encounters with the animals in your life fill you with a sense of wonder, connection, and peace that borders on the spiritual.

- If you consider yourself an atheist, what is your "religion?" What gives your life meaning? What do you believe in? What are your values? What takes you beyond yourself and allows you to have a positive impact on the world? Perhaps you have never thought of yourself in this way before.

---

21. Peterson, cited in Job and Shawchuck, *A Guide to Prayer,* 322–23.

- How does it feel to think of yourself as spiritual even though you do not believe in God? Write your answers to these questions in your journal if you wish. What are some practices you might engage in that express your own personal spirituality? Find ways to fit these practices into your life more often.

HEALING PRACTICE 4

Humans throughout the centuries have endured great suffering. Many of the psalms are written by people who are crying out to God in the midst of their deepest pain. This type of psalm is called a lament. Read Psalm 31:9–16. I'm sure you can relate to the feelings and experiences of the psalmist David in this passage. Another lament of David is found in Psalm 6.

- Try writing your own lament. Sometimes it helps to write about your wounds and brokenness in a way that validates the depth of what you have experienced. Try putting some words on paper that express your anguish over your abuse.

- What you do with this writing is up to you. You might pray with it, share it with a trusted friend, pastor, counselor, or spiritual director, keep it in a special place, or choose instead to destroy it.

2

Why Does God Hate Me?

*"Look, O Lord, and consider, for I am despised."—*LAMENTATIONS 1:11B

I still remember the first time a survivor of severe and prolonged incest asked me, "Why does God hate me?" I also remember that despite my many reassurances, there were no words that could convince her that she was and always had been inside the circle of God's love. I have learned since then that when a client asks this difficult question, it is imperative that I first validate that it must indeed have felt like that to them before I enter into the heady territory of the theology of a loving God. There are many factors that contribute to this conviction that sexual abuse victims are reviled by God. These include the actions of their abusers, the deep shame that is experienced by almost all survivors of abuse, and the perception that their desperate prayers for the abuse to end went unanswered.

Perpetrator Behavior

A long-term client of mine, Susan, was only eight years old when she remembers waking up one morning to excruciating pain. Her stepfather was in bed with her, not for the first time, and it felt like he was tearing her in half. She wanted to cry out but knew that would invite even greater pain, so she held herself silent and still until the waking nightmare stopped. Eventually, her abuser did stop, roll away from her, and begin dressing. It was then

19

that Susan saw the suit he was wearing, the shiny dress shoes he pulled onto his feet—not everyday attire for a blue-collar worker. He walked to the door, turned to wink at her with a cautionary finger to his lips, and strolled casually down the hall. Her stepfather was on his way to church.

It is experiences like these that can cause survivors of sexual abuse to develop a belief that God hates them. When perpetrators are churchgoing people—people who teach Sunday school, sing in the choir, say grace at every meal, and in general put on an outward persona of piety and devotion to God—a child will naturally believe that God is on the side of the perpetrator. A child cannot understand that people can appear to be good followers of their religion in public and still perpetrate evil, unrighteous acts in private. They may assume that the abusive episodes are part and parcel of what faithful believers do. And when the abuse continues unabated, it seems logical to think this is the way it is supposed to be, that God knows about and condones the abuse, because it is being carried out by a "righteous" person. Something that hurts this much, horrifies and wounds more profoundly than anything the child has ever experienced can only be the product of God's indifference, anger, or malice. If the child comes to believe this, the natural conclusion is that God hates him or her. Children usually do not have the cognitive ability to make sense of what is happening, to view the abuse as something that is wrong with their abuser rather than with themselves, or to know that God is deeply offended by both the abuser's actions and hypocrisy. A child's belief that God is on the side of the abuser is further reinforced when the abuser tells him or her directly that this is so:

> Perpetrators of abuse in religious households will frequently use religious language, symbols, and concepts to justify their abusive acts to their victims. Christian teachings on suffering are sometimes summoned to support violent acts. The assumption is that since God is just and merciful, suffering is the result of sin . . . . The abused child is led to believe that her suffering is punishment for her sins.[1]

Another confusing and troubling behavior by the offender occurs when, during the throes of sexual pleasure, he cries out, "Oh, my God!" Susan often told me, in the midst of a flashback, that her stepfather prayed while he committed his atrocities. To a child, the words "Oh, my God"

---

1. Driskell, "Traumatized Persons," 28.

sound very much like a prayer. Given a child's complete innocence about sexual passion, how can he or she understand that this outcry is not a prayer at all? It is only as sexually active adults that we have the frame of reference to know the difference between prayer and sexual passion. Not only are children unable to comprehend what is happening to them, they are also developmentally incapable of verbalizing their confusion to another adult. Without any other point of reference, this intense expression of physical pleasure that seems addressed to God connects God even more directly to the pain this child is experiencing. This confusion may leave a victim feeling completely outside the scope of God's love and alone in a world in which God is there for the perpetrator but certainly not for them.

Sometimes, the adults in their lives who should have protected them act in ways that further isolate them from a loving and comforting God. Susan would often try to hide from her stepfather during times when she had come to learn he would want sex. Sometimes she was successful and other times not. One particular day, her predator found her hiding in a closet. Because she had delayed his gratification, he was angry and determined to punish her for her willfulness. Knowing that nothing she did could stop him from his horrible revenge, she sought to find something other than the abuse to focus on. In the next room, she could hear the TV on and tried to listen to it as a distraction. At first, she couldn't make out the words, but gradually, it got louder and louder. Her mother was watching her favorite televangelist, and the words of the Lord's Prayer came clearly through the wall. It was only later that Susan realized her mother must have been turning up the volume in order to drown out the sounds of her own husband assaulting her daughter. This seemed to Susan to be even more evidence that God was on the side of both the perpetrator and other adults that allowed the abuse to happen.

It is not uncommon in cases of incest for other family members to know or suspect that the abuse is taking place. There are many reasons why these adults might ignore, deny, or hide from what is happening to the children in their care. Some of them may have been abused themselves. They may believe that sexual abuse is an inevitable part of childhood, and even though they don't like it, that they are powerless to stop it. Their deep shame about their own abuse may keep them from speaking up or defending the innocent victim. Others may be afraid of the abuser or of the disruption that would occur in the family if they were to try to stop the abuse. Susan's mother was afraid of her husband's temper and convinced that she could not raise her daughter and two other children on her own. Regardless of the reason, one of the ways in which these adult family members sometimes block out their knowledge of the abuse is through their religion. They might believe that if they just pray enough, everything will be all right, or that the abuse is truly a deserved punishment for some perceived sin. Or they may immerse themselves in their church in order to atone for their own guilt about not protecting the victim. Either way, the impact on the child is the same. There is yet another adult in her life that seems to be within the fold of God's love, while the child feels as though she has been cast into the outer darkness, because that person is failing to acknowledge, intervene, or stop the abuse, thereby giving tacit permission for it to continue. Even in cases where family members truly know nothing of the abuse, the fact that they continue on with their normal lives, especially their religious lives, underscores for the victim that he is invisible and forgotten.

HEALING PRACTICE 1

In the New Testament, Jesus spoke out strongly against the Pharisees and other church leaders who led outwardly pious lives, yet were corrupt and dishonest in their business dealings and treated people of lower status with contempt. Read Luke 6:41–42 and Matthew 6:2–6, 16–18. Jesus saw through the supposedly righteous acts of these people and into their hearts, which desired not righteousness but worldly importance, riches, and the admiration of their peers. If this is the case, do you think Jesus would be able to see the dark acts of your abuser beneath the outward show of Christian piety? Based on the Scripture you read, how do you think Jesus would feel about that? How do you think he would feel about the so-called Christians who knew about your abuse and did nothing?

Shame and Punishment

My work with abuse survivors over the years has taught me that shame is universal, deeply felt, and not easily shaken. Their offenders have told them repeatedly, "You make me do this." A child might not have any idea what she has done to deserve this punishment, but she clearly understands that she is being punished for something. Over and over in Scripture, especially in the Old Testament, God's people try to make sense of calamity and misfortune by believing it to be God's punishment. When children attend church or

Sunday school and hear these stories or psalms read out loud, the message comes through loud and clear—bad things happen to bad people. In the child's developmental stage of thought, which is concrete and absolute, this makes sense to him.[2] Being the recipient of such horrendous punishment as sexual violation therefore equates in his mind to offenses so horrible that God must indeed hate him.

Another thing victims are often told is that they invited or wanted the abuse. They have no idea what they may have done to send that signal, but they feel shame about it nonetheless. The idea that their perpetrator might be saying this so that the guilt-ridden child will not report the abuse doesn't enter their mind. Nor do they imagine that the offender could be attempting to justify the abusive behavior in his own mind. And the fact that many victims experience physical pleasure despite their desire for the abuse to stop merely confirms their belief that they are willing participants in something shameful and wrong. They feel betrayed by their bodies and unable to control their response to what the abuser is doing. As mentioned in chapter 1, children of abuse often learn to masturbate in order to self-soothe, and their participation in an activity so similar to the abuse reinforces the idea that they must actually want to be sexually violated in this way. It is so hard for them to believe that the offending adult is the only one who is responsible for the abuse, regardless of the sexual feelings they experience. Typically, no one has ever suggested such a possibility to them, and they are left to make sense of this heinous behavior on their own. The shame deepens, and if they have been raised in a religious household where misdeeds have been referred to as sin, then sin they have, and it is a sin which merits severe punishment in their eyes.

HEALING PRACTICE 2

In some of the healing stories of the Gospels, Jesus refutes the long-held belief that misfortune, illness, and disability were the result of sin, and in Matthew 5:45, he teaches that rain falls on the righteous and the unrighteous without distinguishing between them. Healing your shame and sense of being worthy of punishment begins with believing that sometimes bad things do happen to good people. It was your abuser alone, not God or you, who was responsible for the painful abuse you experienced. Imagine yourself in a safe and peaceful place. It might be someplace familiar to

---

2. An in-depth discussion of developmental stages will be presented in chapter 3.

you as a place of refuge or it might be a place that exists only in your imagination—a lush, walled garden or a castle on a cloud, drifting through a clear, blue sky. Establish yourself in this place with all of your senses, imagining the sights, sounds, smells, and sensations of it. Imagine that you can feel a loving presence all around you. Imagine a voice speaking to you with great kindness. If your abuser was a male, it might be helpful for this divine voice to be female. These are the words you might hear spoken: "The abuse you suffered was not your fault. You did not deserve the things that happened to you. You could not help the things you were forced to do." Hear God saying to you, "I see the goodness of your heart and would never punish you. I did not bring about, nor desire, your suffering. You are loved just as you are." Write down your feelings about this experience. It may take several repetitions of this exercise before you begin to believe that it might be true.

Unanswered Prayer

Many, many victims of abuse have prayed fervently to God to make their torment stop. For some, this is a last-ditch effort after trying desperately to get parents, teachers, or others to listen, believe, and come to their aid. I have heard stories of children who told their mothers that their father or grandfather or babysitter was touching them, only to be assured that they must be mistaken or that the child was to blame for provoking the abuse. Some victims were even beaten for daring to speak of the abuse out loud. So when these children turn to God, it is with the knowledge that there is nowhere else to go. When their impassioned pleas do not result in an end to the abuse, the only thing they can believe is that God chose not to act on their behalf. By the time Nicole was a teenager, having suffered repeated abuse from multiple offenders, she had come to believe that God had "ditched" her, that divine intervention was something that happened for others, but not for her.

In Sunday school, children are taught that God answers prayer. When they hear stories in church of miracles and healings and other answered prayers, they are left to wonder why God is not answering *their* prayer. Children are too young to understand the nature of prayer or the myriad, often indirect ways in which God answers prayer. They do not comprehend that abusers choose to live outside the will of God, and that the gift of free will limits God's ability to act. And even if they could understand it, there may be no one who genuinely comprehends their suffering or, unfortunately, cares enough to explain it to them. All these children know is that the abuse continues, and they feel utterly alone in their belief that they are despised by God.

HEALING PRACTICE 3

When people talk to me about their sense of being abandoned by God, I help them explore the possibility that God brought angels into their lives, people whose caring presence helped them survive years of abuse and pain. Almost without exception, survivors are able to name an aunt or uncle, a grandparent, a special teacher, a friend's mother, or a neighbor—someone with whom they felt safe, who made them feel special and gave them appropriate affection. I believe that these people were God's answer to the abused child's prayers.

- Name the person or persons who were your angels.

- Write about your memories of them, the way they made you feel, how they treated you differently from those who hurt you.

- If they are still alive, find a way to thank them for being there. You don't have to tell them about the abuse (unless they already know) in order to let them know how much they meant to you. If they are no longer living, write a letter to them sharing your feelings and put it in a special place, possibly with a picture of them or some other memento.

HEALING PRACTICE 4

People throughout history have cried out to God from the depths of their despair and felt that their prayers were unanswered. Sometimes it is helpful to read their words and know that you are not alone in feeling the way you do. Read Psalm 88. The person who wrote this psalm lived thousands of years ago yet may be echoing some of the same thoughts and feelings you have lived through during the many long, dark nights when God felt far, far away.

- If you wrote your own psalm of lament to God in chapter 1, reread it now.

- Ask God to help you feel that God is listening.

- Is there anyone in your life who has listened to you? If so, how did that make you feel?

- Even if they were unable to change your circumstances, was it enough that they truly heard you?

3

"When I Was a Child…"

The Impact of Child Sexual Abuse on Spiritual Development

> *"When I was a child, I spoke like a child, I thought like a child, I reasoned like a child; when I became an adult, I put an end to childish ways."*
> —1 CORINTHIANS 13:11 *(NRSV)*

Since the early twentieth century, psychologists and educators have been attempting to explain human behavior by identifying and describing the various stages through which individuals progress from birth to death. Piaget, Erikson, and Kohlberg are among those most well-known for their ground-breaking work in developing models of cognitive, emotional, and moral development. Borrowing heavily from the ideas of these experts, James Fowler, in his book, *Stages of Faith*, outlines the normal development of spiritual faith—from the naïve faith of early childhood to the rule-bound and conventional beliefs of later childhood and adolescence to critique, reflection, and, ultimately and ideally, wisdom in later years.[1] Unfortunately, the development of victims of child sexual abuse is anything but normal. Psychologists and other mental health professionals have come to understand that trauma, in addition to its many other negative effects, also has a profound impact on human development. In other words, emotional, cognitive, moral, and social development is often severely compromised by

---

1. Fowler, *Stages of Faith*, 11.

27

traumatic events. This means that, while normal physical and psychomotor development continues, the victim can get stuck in an early stage of mental and emotional maturity—in whatever stage they were when the abuse began. Even when cognitive thinking skills develop normally so the child can learn such things as algebra, physics, and analytical thought, their emotional life and belief system may retain a childlike quality. This arrested development impacts the way they perceive themselves, others, and the world around them. It impacts relationships. It also severely hampers a normal and healthy passage through the stages of faith and a healthy relationship with God.

The task of faith development is to find meaning, order, and coherence in our lives.[2] We are all a composite of our own experiences. They shape us. They determine how we feel about ourselves and others, how we make sense of the world, and who we think God is. Normally, these ideas and feelings will change with us as we grow. For example, our belief in Santa Claus and the Easter Bunny eventually grows into an understanding that our parents were the true culprits, striving to protect our childhood delight in all things magical. However, trauma causes childlike beliefs and understandings of the world to become static, almost frozen in time, despite subsequent experiences that might ordinarily further growth and maturity. In regard to faith development, catastrophic events such as sexual abuse can create a significant shift in the victim's image of God and then freeze it. Without the outside intervention of a loving adult, therapist, or spiritual guide, the potential for spiritual growth to help the victim find comfort and meaning is lost.

Infancy

Some believe that in infancy, we are fresh from God, only recently departed from our dwelling place within God's spirit.[3] There is an innate faith that already exists just waiting to be shaped. James Fowler calls this primal or undifferentiated faith.[4] Our very first unconscious images of God are shaped by the parents upon whom babies depend to meet their every need. Infants' parents or primary caregivers are their entire world, so affectionate and attentive parents will usually contribute to a later image of God that is

2. Ibid., 24.

3. Scharf, "Stages of Faith," 4.

4. Fowler, *Stages of Faith*, 121.

likewise loving and available. While abuse that happens in infancy cannot be remembered, it is nonetheless likely to have profound impact on a child's later images of God. The image of God as a loving father that is portrayed in many a Sunday school class might instead become the frightening specter of a parent who, at best, utterly failed in the most fundamental way to protect his child, and at worst, was capable of the violation of a helpless infant.

Early Childhood

In early childhood, from roughly the ages of two to six, children relate to the world through their five senses. It is a narrow world consisting of people and objects they can see, hear, taste, smell, and touch. Abstract concepts, such as love, freedom, or responsibility are not understood, because they have no physically perceivable reference. While young children might not understand the concept of authority, they do know that grown-ups are boss. They will often automatically comply with the wishes of someone older and bigger, and they fear getting into trouble if they don't. Since parents are usually focused on getting their children to behave at this age, toddlers quickly learn that being "good" leads to rewards and being "bad" leads to punishment. Yet there is little understanding of cause and effect, so if a child gets in trouble for spilling milk, she might know she was bad but not what she did to cause the punishment.

Children at this age can ask a hundred questions a day in their efforts to make sense of the world, but when faced with something beyond the known and familiar, they will often fill in the gaps of their understanding with magical thinking. Because their world revolves around them, they may end up believing that they somehow cause everything that happens. In a lovely children's story entitled *The Puppy Who Chased the Sun*, a puppy rises before sunrise every morning and begins to bark. And every morning the sun comes up.[5] The puppy believes that his barking causes the sun to rise, so he is utterly perplexed when one day the sun does not come up at all. Ultimately, the puppy discovers that the sun has been obscured by clouds. This is an example of the kind of associations children make between their behavior and the events in their lives, which are often unrelated.

In terms of faith development, children from two to six are attracted to mythic stories of good and evil in the Bible. They have absolute trust in what they are taught by their parents and teachers as the ultimate

5. Grand, *Puppy Who Chased the Sun*.

authorities. Their image of God is mythical and all-powerful. When asked, they will tell you that God created everything, knows everything, is able to be everywhere, and gives us what we ask for. God is a magician, Superman, the candy man, and Santa Claus all rolled into one.

Now imagine what it might be like if a child of this age was to experience sexual abuse. Because his sense of right and wrong is based on the presence of reward or punishment, a victim will automatically believe that he did something wrong that resulted in the abuse. Since it is not conceivable to doubt authority, it does not occur to him that the abuser is doing something wrong. Nor can he imagine that God feels any differently about the abuse than he does, which is that the victim must deserve it. When abused children go to Sunday school and hear the stories of Shadrach, Meshach, and Abednego being saved from the fiery furnace or Daniel being delivered from the lion's den, they might wonder why God doesn't save them from their own ferocious predator. The stories show that God is capable of rescuing but doesn't in their case. Sometimes the only conclusion a sexually abused child can come to is that God condones her abuse as punishment for "being bad." Since, as discussed, trauma arrests normal development, an adult survivor might be able to acknowledge the concept that God loves everyone yet still be stuck in the belief that God does not love *her*.

Sylvia is a sixty-year-old woman who was molested by her older brother from the time she was five years old. Sylvia was raised Catholic, but no longer practices her religion. Despite her lack of attendance at Mass, she still believes in God and particularly in angels. She talks about God's presence in her life in a very vague and magical way, which is very typical of early childhood understandings of God. She believes that the good things that happen to her are God's reward for good behavior. She also fears that she will be punished for her extramarital affair and her inability to forgive those who have wronged her. Sylvia's image of God and her focus on reward and punishment make it clear that her spiritual growth became stunted in the stage during which she was first abused. She and survivors like her will have difficulty relating to God in a way that promotes healing and a more mature faith.

Later Childhood

From approximately age seven through twelve, children's thought processes are orderly, predictable, and chronological. They are more able to make connections between their behavior and its consequences, but they do expect those consequences to be fair. They accept that there are rules they need to follow and that failure to do so results in punishment. During this stage of faith development, children are focused on following the rules of their religion. They do not yet understand an abstract concept like grace, so they tend to believe that heaven and relationship with God must be earned. To children of that age, God takes on human characteristics and is seen primarily as loving parent and benevolent ruler. Some may have begun to question whether God is truly all-powerful, because they are old enough to see things happening in the world that seem confusing if God is really in charge of everything as they have previously assumed. However, when they are unable to explain events, they fall back on the belief that things must happen for a reason.

When sexual abuse occurs during this time period, it is likely that the victims will become even more entrenched in their rule-bound approach to life. Their rigidity applies both to themselves and others. They inhabit a black-and-white world with absolutely no shades of gray. These people will become Bible literalists and possibly quite intolerant of anyone who fails to abide by the principles of their religion. At the same time, they bear a great burden of shame. Assuming the abuse happened for a reason, that God in the role of ruler allowed it to happen, they believe they must have deserved it. God's presumed judgment prevents them from feeling worthy of being in God's presence.

Terri, whose grandfather molested her for years during her childhood, has an image of God as judge or stern father figure that is disapproving and punitive. She ascribes absolutely to the rules of faith, holding both herself and others to this impossibly high standard. Because she works so hard at following biblical precepts, it bothers her when others do not, yet seem to lead blessed lives. When a co-worker developed hepatitis C due to drug use as a youth, Terri secretly believed that this woman deserved her fate. Later, Terri suffered a health crisis of her own, which caused her to wonder what she had done to deserve this punishment from God. She beat herself up over even the smallest infraction of the rules. Mercy was not a word in her vocabulary. Her abuser had never showed her mercy, and she couldn't imagine that God would either. It is no wonder that she is unable to feel close to God or trust that God is a loving, forgiving divinity.

Adolescence

While teenagers have reached full physical maturity and have acquired advanced thinking skills, their experience of the world is not yet adequate to classify them as adults. Their lack of experience beyond the current boundaries of their lives can create self-doubt and anxieties about the future for which they are not yet prepared. Even so, their capacity for analytical and abstract thought makes them able to learn and retain a large body of knowledge, to think logically, and to discern meaning from the events of their lives. While they might not use these skills often or well, the capability still exists. Adolescents are beginning to develop the ability to view things from multiple perspectives, perhaps because their social world has begun to expand beyond the boundaries of family, and they are exposed to many more points of view than in earlier years. Peers begin to take on greater importance as a teenager embarks on the process of separation and individuation from family. Friends become people with whom one shares one's deepest thoughts and feelings rather than merely same-age companions with whom to participate in mutual activities. Teenagers, as most parents know, are also a bundle of contradictions—idealistic, yet judgmental; conformist, yet fighting for independence. This is a time of turmoil and of the struggle for identity.

The faith that emerges during this stage is a reflection of their cognitive and social development. Adolescents are deeply sensitive to the expectations of others, especially their peers. They need to see themselves mirrored in others in order to feel OK about who they are. This leads them to dress, act, and believe just like their peers. Their faith beliefs are beginning to be more sophisticated, but they are not yet confident enough to examine or question their faith. Adolescent idealism often leads to involvement in service and mission projects. Church is a place of community and relationship, and this focus on relationship extends to their image of God. God is no longer a magical figure like a fairy godmother, nor is God the distant, powerful, and judgmental deity of earlier states. Instead, God is more personal, a being who guides and supports. Later teens may even see God as their closest friend, one who accompanies them through life.[6]

Trauma that occurs during adolescence has the potential to cast doubt on all that the victim has believed and counted on since childhood, thus leading them into despair. As with many issues related to sexual abuse, it

6. Scharf, "Stages of Faith," 9.

32

may also have the opposite effect of increased faith. It is possible that a teenager from a strong faith background may be able to turn to their personal relationship with God as a source of comfort and hope. This is supported by a study by Chandy et al. that found female adolescents with a higher level of religiosity suffered fewer negative effects from their abuse.[7] Despite this, experiences of abuse may freeze them at their current stage of faith development, preventing them from moving into a deeper and more reflective spirituality that comes from examining the teachings of the church and formulating a faith that expands beyond familiar structures to become an expression of a more profound truth.

Jessica grew up in a very religious family. Her father was a Baptist minister, and her mother directed the church choir. At the age of 17, she had never experienced any kind of abuse. She was happy, healthy, an excellent student, and very involved in her church. Jessica was on a cross-country red-eye flight after a mission trip when the man seated next to her took advantage of her drowsiness to reach under her blanket and fondle her. Her astonishment and fear caused her to freeze, and it was several minutes before she was able to alert the flight attendant to what was happening. In the aftermath of this event, despite being severely traumatized, Jessica was able to sense God's presence with her for support, comfort, and strength. Her ability to function academically and socially was significantly compromised, but her faith remained intact. Imaging Christ seated in the courtroom with her allowed her to get through the difficult trial, and she stated that her relationship with God was closer than ever. What remains to be seen is whether her faith will continue to develop and mature beyond the boundaries of her current conventional beliefs.

HEALING PRACTICE 1

Can you identify which of the four development stages you were in when your abuse began? Do you see yourself in the descriptions of faith in any of these stages? If not, that's OK. These are just general categories, and not everyone follows the same pattern as they grow and develop. If you do identify with one particular stage, take some time to think about your beliefs at that age compared to what they are now. Has your faith grown over time or does it feel stuck in that earlier stage of development? In what ways are your current beliefs harmful or helpful as you seek to heal from the abuse you suffered? Can you consider the possibility that there are other

7. Chandy et al., "Female Adolescents," 503–18.

ways of believing in and perceiving God? Open yourself to these possibilities by attending a different church or reading about other religions. Talk to people from different faith traditions to hear how they believe and what God means to them. Remember that truth is relative. There is no "one size fits all" way of believing. The purpose of this exercise is not to change your beliefs but to help you come to your own beliefs through a process of examination and questioning. And everyone can benefit from growing in faith.

4

"Lord, Help My Unbelief"
Obstacles on the Path to Faith

"But if you can do anything, take pity on us and help us." "If you can?" said Jesus. "Everything is possible for him who believes." Immediately the boy's father exclaimed, "I do believe; help me overcome my unbelief."
—EXCERPTS FROM MARK 9:22B–24

Like the father of the dying daughter in the Scripture above, survivors of child sexual abuse struggle with questions of faith. Webster's New World Dictionary cites the following definitions of the word "believe": "1. to take as true, real, etc. 2. to have confidence in a statement or promise of (another person). 3. to have trust or confidence (in). 4. to have religious faith."[1] James Fowler, in his book, *Stages of Faith*, states, "Faith involves an alignment of the heart or will, a commitment of loyalty and trust."[2] Most sexual abuse survivors don't really have a problem with the first meaning of the word "believe" when it comes to God. Many do believe there is a God, but when it comes to applying the subsequent meanings of the word, their faith starts to break down. Confidence, trust, commitment, promises—these are all immensely frightening words for someone whose body and spirit have been appallingly violated by their abusers. It would almost

1. *Webster's New World Dictionary*, 81.
2. Fowler, *Stages of Faith*, 11.

be better for them if they didn't believe at all, for their struggle is in the tension between belief and unbelief. Survivors would like to believe in the same way as others do, would like to trust in God and in the promises of Scripture, but the very nature and impact of their abuse makes this nearly impossible.

In addition, those who have suffered sexual abuse struggle to feel worthy of their place with God or in God's church. Many years ago, there was a popular beer commercial featuring Bob Uecker in which he stood shivering on a dark, snowy street outside a tavern that was serving the beer being advertised. He had somehow gotten locked out, and as he stood with his face pressed against the window and watched the people in the warm, bright bar dancing and laughing, his plaintive cry was, "They're sure having a good time in there." This is what I imagine it is like for survivors who are part of a faith community. They attend the worship services, the Bible studies, the potluck dinners, but they feel locked out somehow. Though their body is present in the church building, their soul feels removed from it all, outside on a cold, dark, and lonely street, pressing their face against the glass and watching all those people who are inside. Those others seem to be basking in the light and warmth of God's love, enjoying the spiritual party, where blessings flow and true believers have access to an abundance of peace and joy. Survivors may know intellectually that all are invited, but they seem to have lost the invitation, and they don't know the code that unlocks the door. This chapter relates some of the factors which contribute to their crisis of faith.

HEALING PRACTICE 1

Many survivors are extremely troubled by their doubts and their difficulty in believing. They assume that faith is supposed to be absolute and unquestioning. This is far from the truth. In personal letters released after Mother Theresa's death, she revealed her own period of darkness in which she doubted God's very existence. Kathleen Norris, well-known author on issues of faith, relates a story in which she was sharing her own doubts with an old monk and was surprised by his response: "Doubt is merely the seed of faith, a sign that faith is alive and ready to grow."[3] I believe this to be true. Doubt itself can be sacred, revealing a desire to believe, yet not knowing how to get there. Perhaps the key is in not giving up

3. Norris, *Amazing Grace*, 63.

but continuing to wrestle with issues of faith until the seed begins to sprout and grow. This may take a long time, but God is patient.

- Can you be patient with yourself? Can you consider the idea that your doubt is merely a way station on the path to faith?

- It may be helpful to use the metaphor of the seed as you make your first halting steps on the journey toward faith. Do you desire faith? Do you believe that a seed of faith already exists within you? If you want it to grow, what might you do to tend and water this seed? What conditions will help it to grow?

- Journal your thoughts or draw a picture of the garden, orchard, forest, or other habitat in which your seed will grow.

Depression

Several of the symptoms and long-term effects of having been sexually abused also have significant impact on a survivor's ability to connect with God and/or the church. One of these is depression, which is fairly common among abuse survivors. Depression casts a pall over the sufferer's life and makes everything appear dull, gray, and lifeless. It has a profound impact on one's motivation and energy level, making activities that are effortless for others feel like daunting and impossible tasks for one who is depressed. When depressed survivors find themselves unable to participate in the regular activities of the church, which might bring a sense of belonging and peace, they may feel lazy, ashamed, and unworthy of receiving the benefits of faith. This unfounded guilt, another symptom of depression, makes living a righteous life seem impossible, and making the attempt is viewed as just one more opportunity to fail to meet the perceived expectations of God and the church. Meanwhile, fellow church members are reading Scripture and praying daily (or so it seems), serving on committees, feeding the homeless at the local shelter, and singing in the choir. When faced with the seeming impossibility of measuring up to this standard, how easy it would be for hopelessness to set in!

Survivors of sexual abuse tend to experience extreme pessimism and have great difficulty believing that anything good could ever happen to them. This includes having a positive "God experience." Since depression impacts their ability to experience enjoyment, they can't imagine the joy, peace, or sense of God's presence that others may describe when they are praying or meditating. Their self-critical logic leads them to the conclusion that they are doing something wrong or that God doesn't love them enough to reach out to them in such a tangible and profound way. Fortunately, God has incredible power to sometimes break through this miasma of darkness and negativity.

Rachel, who experienced a date rape on her seventeenth birthday, held the belief that while God loved most people of faith, God certainly did not love her. Prayer was almost impossible for her, and the last time she could remember a sense of God's presence was as a young child. She felt like an outsider in her strictly religious family and in the fundamentalist church they attended. She did not take communion because of her shame over certain behaviors she practiced that were contrary to church teachings. Yet during Lent one year, she attended an exhibit of paintings of Christ that was sponsored by her church. As she sat on a bench near one of the paintings, she couldn't take her eyes off the image of Christ holding out his hand with the nail wound clearly visible. It seemed that he was looking straight at her, and the expression on his face was pure compassion. She became aware of tears streaming down her face and a feeling of being surrounded by immense love and acceptance. She felt an assurance that God was indeed with her in that moment and was promising to be with her through all the moments to come. While this incident did not resolve all of her problems, it did allow her to access her faith as a support in her healing. She began to pray and journal regularly and no longer questioned God's deep love for her.

Another factor in this pessimism is actually a symptom of post-traumatic stress disorder—a foreshortened sense of the future.[4] This means that sufferers are unable to imagine a future at all, much less a positive one. They often believe that they will die young, and if that is the case, they see no reason to bother working toward a hopeful future. A happy and healthy life or the rewards of heaven seem equally out of reach to them. Participating fully in spiritual practices, worship services, Bible studies, and other church activities that might enhance their lives seems futile to them and requires more energy than they feel like they have.

HEALING PRACTICE 2

The problem of not believing that you belong in your church or in God's kingdom is painful and difficult to overcome. You may

4. *Diagnostic and Statistical Manual IV,* 428.

think that you are neither good enough nor worthy enough to be included with other people of faith. Yet there are many biblical passages that refute such beliefs, among them these verses from I Cor 1:27–28, "But God chose the foolish things of the world to shame the wise; God chose the weak things of the world to shame the strong. He chose the lowly things of this world and the despised things . . . ." What this means is that our brokenness does not cause God to pull away the welcome mat from the door of the kingdom. We do not have to be perfect Christians, with perfect lives and perfect faith in order to belong to the club. There is no secret handshake that you missed out on while you were being abused. Michael Yaconelli, in his book, *Messy Spirituality*, puts it this way:

> What landed Jesus on the cross was the preposterous idea that common, ordinary, broken, screwed-up people could be godly! What drove Jesus' enemies crazy were his criticisms of the "perfect" religious people and his acceptance of the imperfect nonreligious people. The shocking implication of Jesus' ministry is that anyone can be spiritual.[5]

This means even sex abuse survivors.

- There are many stories in the Bible of Jesus reaching out to the outcasts of society, people who were rejected, scorned, or living in ways that were unacceptable to the righteous status quo. These included women, the unclean, anyone who was demon-possessed, tax collectors, adulterers, and sinners. Read some of the following passages: John 4:4–30, Luke 7:36–50, Luke 8:42–48, Luke 13:10–17, Luke 15:1–2, Luke 17:11–19, Luke 19:1–10.

- Perhaps you can journal about these passages or write a story in which you put yourself in the place of one of these biblical characters.

- Imagine what it might feel like to encounter Christ in that way, for example, as the woman with the issue of blood. What would you feel as you were pushing through the crowd? Afraid? Hopeful? What would you want to say to Jesus when he turned toward you? Imagine his healing power coursing

5. Yaconelli, *Messy Spirituality*, 21.

into your soul. What would it be like to feel his loving attention and know that you are accepted by him just as you are? How would that change you?

Control Issues

Those who have experienced child sexual abuse know what it means to have all personal choice taken from them. Abusers exerted the ultimate control over their bodies, their emotions, and their behaviors, sometimes to the point of controlling whether they lived or died. Terri remembers being choked by hands, ropes, and the like on many occasions, having the barrel of a gun inserted into her vagina, and any number of other life-threatening actions. Expecting her imminent death was commonplace. Her perpetrator did indeed hold her life in his hands on these occasions. Yet when he caught her attempting suicide, he became intensely angry and punished her cruelly for daring to try such a thing. The message was that he alone had control of her life and death.

Both Nicole's mother and one of her male perpetrators exerted absolute control over her urination and bowels. She was told when to go to the bathroom and was punished if she went without permission. She was expected to hold her urine and/or bowel movements for hours if they failed to give her permission to go. Of course, she was also punished for wetting or soiling herself—a no-win situation. To this day, she struggles with incontinence, because she learned to ignore her own body signals.

Not all survivors will have experienced such extreme abuse, but they do know how it feels to have control taken away from them, whether for a few minutes, hours, months, or years. Now consider some of the words that are spoken of frequently in faith settings—surrender, submission, trust, obedience, yielding, and letting go. How difficult do you imagine those words might be for someone for whom submission meant allowing another person to sexually violate them? In fact, yielding themselves to God is perhaps the most frightening thing that many survivors can contemplate. If this is the criterion for membership in the kingdom of God, then count them out! And as for God's plan and God's will? Survivors are all too familiar with their abuser's plans and their abuser's will for them to imagine a divine and loving will or a plan that is meant to "prosper you and not to harm you, plans to give you hope and a future" (Jer 29:11). Allowing anyone to exert control over their lives is next to impossible for them to do. They need desperately to maintain control of themselves, their behaviors, thoughts, and emotions, even their environment and their friends and family.

Despite their difficulty in trusting God and submitting to God's will, it is not uncommon for survivors to cling to the rules of faith—the commandments, laws, and doctrines that govern behavior. Rules give them a sense of control. Here is a concrete prescription they can follow, a road map for meeting expectations and getting things right. Their membership in the family of God is under their control, and if they fail, then it is not because someone changed the rules or arbitrarily decided they couldn't belong. These laws are also a way for them to feel OK about themselves. When they are following church doctrine to the letter while people around them are falling short, it even allows them to feel superior to others for short periods of time. To them, rules are good. Rules provide structure. But ask them to actually surrender to the Divine, and they will look at you like a deer caught in the headlights.

Survivors often have such anxiety that it causes them to need to be in control of themselves at all times. This means that they must always be on high alert, ever vigilant to signs of danger or threat. They are usually quite unable to relax, even while sitting in a pew at church. Someone might sit next to them whose physical characteristics, cologne, or manner of speaking reminds them of their abuser, causing even greater tension and further distracting them from the worship service that is unfolding around them. Sometimes, just closing one's eyes for prayer feels like a loss of control. And a simple activity like passing the peace of Christ can be fraught with intense anxiety for one who can barely tolerate the touch of others. Peace is the last thing they are feeling at a time like this. Their constant tension means that survivors don't feel safe enough to open themselves to spiritual moments in church, just one more way in which a connection to God and others is out of reach. They are unable to achieve a sense of worship or community. Even church activities that are more informal and that others might perceive as less threatening may still be difficult for the survivor of abuse. While they might be particularly efficient at organizing the annual church picnic, letting down their guard enough to truly fellowship with others during the picnic is another matter. Such events might feel too chaotic and overwhelming for survivors who need to have control over themselves and their environment in order to feel safe.

HEALING PRACTICE 3

If you are someone who finds it difficult to relax in church, if you find yourself constantly scanning your surroundings for potential danger, then church may not be the place where you can allow yourself to experience God's presence, at least at first. Sometimes it helps to find a safe place where you don't have to watch for signs of danger and can let go just a little in order to have a spiritual experience. Where is your safe place? Many of my clients feel safest in small, closed-in spaces such as closets, corners, or hidey holes. You might remember Nicole, the survivor I described in chapter 1, who often sleeps underneath her dining table. Sometimes she drapes a blanket over it so that she feels even more protected. Others prefer to be somewhere outdoors in a large open space where they can see for long distances. In fact, nature is a more beautiful sanctuary than anything humankind could ever design. Thomas Merton writes, "My worship is a blue sky and ten thousand crickets in the deep wet hay of the field. My vow is the silence under their song."[6] Wherever your safe place is, it needs to be a place where you can breathe, where you can feel the tension in your body begin to relax, where you can pay more attention to God and less attention to perceived dangers.

- Plan a time when you can go to your special place without being rushed or distracted by the demands of your life. Make yourself as comfortable as possible. At first, just allow yourself to notice what your body feels like when it is in a state of relaxation.

- Focus on your breath, allowing it to slow and deepen. Then turn your mind to God.

- Even when survivors have serious doubts about God and the Bible, they still often have favorite Scriptures—passages that make them feel comforted or loved. Choose one of these Scriptures now to meditate on for a few minutes, pondering what it means to you.

- If you feel able, say a short prayer in which you invite God to be present, and ask God to help you receive the divine presence. Then wait in the silence and see what happens. Don't be discouraged if it feels like nothing is happening. Sometimes things occur in the deepest recesses of our hearts where we

6. Merton, "Cables to the Ace," 400.

are not aware of them. Just because you don't feel anything doesn't mean nothing is happening. Even the act of making the time, being silent, and thinking about God is a good start to developing a spiritual practice that makes you feel connected to something greater than yourself.

Anger

Almost invariably, I find that abuse survivors carry inside them a seething cauldron of rage. This deep anger is sometimes directed inward for not being good enough or strong enough to stop the abuse, especially if they felt physical pleasure while it was happening. But more problematic in terms of their relationships with God and the church is the anger that is aimed at their perpetrators, their families, and others who failed to protect them, as well as at the God who they were taught was always watching over them. They may be bitter and disillusioned at biblical and church teachings that created a false sense that bad things don't happen to good little boys and girls. As children, they may have believed that God would protect them from all harm. Now they wonder where this God, who is supposed to be everywhere, was when the abuse was inflicted and why this all-powerful Being stood by and allowed it to happen. They may even doubt whether God exists at all.

Imagine their thoughts when they hear Bible passages such as these:

- "God is our refuge and strength, an ever-present help in trouble." (Ps 46:1)—"*Why did God abandon me?*"

- "I waited patiently for the Lord; he turned to me and heard my cry. He lifted me out of the slimy pit, out of the mud and mire; he set my feet on a rock and gave me a firm place to stand." (Ps 40:1–2)—"*Why didn't God rescue me?*"

- "For he will deliver the needy who cry out, the afflicted who have no one to help . . . . He will rescue them from oppression and violence, for precious is their blood in his sight." (Ps 72:12, 14)—"*I did cry out! Where was my deliverance?*"

- "He will strike the earth with the rod of his mouth; with the breath of his lips he will slay the wicked." (Isa 11:4b)—"*There was no justice for me, no punishment for my persecutor.*"

Or what about Sunday school song lyrics such as "Jesus loves me, this I know, for the Bible tells me so," or, "Jesus loves the little children, all the children of the world; red and yellow, black and white, they are precious in his sight"? You can imagine survivors thinking, *"I guess I'm just not as precious as the other children,"* or, *"Maybe Jesus loves other children, but he definitely doesn't love me."* When these songs and Scriptures are so incongruent with their abuse experience, it is hard to believe in the goodness of God. In their experience, God was neither a refuge nor a deliverer. God did not lift them out of the pit nor punish their abusers. While church leaders talk about being faithful to God, survivors have no sense that God was faithful to *them*. They become cynical about the message of the Bible and feel that if they cannot trust some of the teachings, they cannot trust any of it. Holocaust survivors are very familiar with this dilemma. As Rubenstein poignantly wonders, "How can Jews believe in an omnipotent God after Auschwitz?"[7] How can anyone who has been through such horrors have faith in something that seems to have failed them so absolutely? And how can those of us who desire to help them fail to validate, understand, and accept their anger?

This kind of acceptance is the first major step for spiritual directors and mental health professionals who are working with sexual abuse survivors. The anger must be validated before one can begin working with the primary emotions that lie beneath it. These emotions may be fear, abandonment, vulnerability, pain, and/or powerlessness. When emotions are this agonizing, anger can be used to put up a protective shell to hold the painful emotions in and the potential hurtfulness of others out.

Without this essential first step, attempts to interpret and explain Scripture in more healing ways or discuss the theology of free will are often met with a blank stare or even more anger. Joanna was outraged at a God who would allow so much suffering in the world, and the concept of free will was appalling to her. It felt like anarchy. If God knew that humans were capable of such evil against one another, then God should have used divine power to control their actions. Humans should not be allowed to make decisions that cause irreparable harm to others. Joanna attempted to participate in a Bible study for a while, trying desperately to find her way back to God, but when the topic of free will came up, she became angry and spoke her mind. Unfortunately, the group was unable to receive and accept her anger. They felt threatened by her hostility and her doubts, and

7. Rubenstein, *After Auschwitz*, 153.

their reaction to her that evening made her feel unwelcome. She never went back.

HEALING PRACTICE 4

Most abuse survivors feel a lot of guilt about their anger at God and the church. Others draw a line in the sand that says to the church, "If you can't handle my anger, that's your problem. If you don't want me here, I'll leave and never come back. It's no skin off my back." Regardless, it's important for you to know that God understands and accepts your anger. The reality is that God is often quite angry at the church as well! God's anger is a righteous anger, one that is deeply offended by the ways in which people hurt and take advantage of others. But God does not lash out in anger; rather, God seeks to find ways to be present to the powerless and victimized while allowing those who misuse power to experience the natural consequences of their actions. We will talk about this more in chapter 7.

- Read about Jesus' rebuke of the Pharisees in Matthew 23:13–39 and his outburst in the temple from Matthew 21:12–13. Jesus was angry at the ways in which the Pharisees twisted the law to their own advantage. When he overturned the tables in the temple, he was protesting the sale of sacrificial animals at such inflated prices that the poor could not afford to fulfill their temple obligations, making them unable to enter God's house. He was telling the money changers that their abusive practices were not acceptable.

- Given Jesus' care for the powerless and disadvantaged of the world, how do you think he would have reacted to discovering your abuser in the act of harming you? Would he have stopped the offender and let him know the abuse was wrong? Would he have gotten your molester away from you? I believe he would. Can you believe it too?

- Based on Matthew 7:1–2, what might Jesus say to people in the church from whom you have felt judgment or criticism for the ways in which you have responded to the abuse or the things you feel about God and faith?

- Reflect on your own anger. Can you give yourself permission to feel the way you do? I often tell my clients that I am glad when they get angry, because it is self-honoring. Your anger says that you deserved better than the abuse you suffered, that it was unacceptable and wrong. Can you then go deeper and identify the feelings that led to your anger? When you become aware of those emotions, talk about them with a trusted friend, therapist, or spiritual director.

Authority Issues and Clergy Abuse

For many survivors, their reasons for distancing themselves from God are the same as the reasons for distancing themselves from the people in their lives. They are wary and afraid of getting hurt again. They have had their trust betrayed over and over again by authority figures that should have protected them, noticed something was wrong, or intervened in some way to stop the abuse from happening. Often, the perpetrator was an authority figure. The long list of people who failed these survivors includes parents, grandparents, aunts and uncles, teachers, police officers, doctors, nurses, daycare providers, neighbors, youth leaders, etc. One of my clients once showed me a picture that she had drawn in grade school that clearly showed her impaled on a bedpost, yet her teacher had failed to see the implications. Nicole remembers running into one of her middle school teachers years later and being told, "Oh, I knew you were being abused, but you were strong. I knew you would get through it." Nicole also recalls the many visits by the police to her apartment because a disturbance had been reported. Despite having been kicked, beaten, and having her head rammed into the wall by her father, the police would give him a verbal slap on the wrist and take the kids to a neighbor for the night to give her parents a "break."

Susan's stepfather often invited his friend, a deputy sheriff, to join him in the abuse that occurred while her mother was away on business. Terri's grandfather and abuser was a city councilman. Sarah's pediatrician had a policy of having children disrobe in the waiting room, and once he got them into an examination room, he took Polaroid pictures of their naked bodies. Mampta's father occasionally included the family doctor in episodes of molestation, and Annie's abuser, having impregnated her, paid for a basement abortion by allowing the doctor sexual access to her immediately afterwards.

Is it any wonder then that many abuse survivors have extreme difficulty in trusting authority? Since God is the ultimate authority figure, distrust automatically gets extended to God as well. As mentioned in chapter 2, oftentimes the victim had prayed for rescue from the abusive situation to no avail. When no help comes, the child can feel abandoned by God and unable to rely on God for help or comfort. The last thing survivors want to do is count on support and protection from the Divine and have the rug pulled out from under them. Making oneself vulnerable to the inevitable failings of someone in a position of power is unthinkable. This distrust of and distancing from God is greatly intensified when the perpetrator is a member of the clergy or other representative of the church.

According to the documentary film *Deliver Us from Evil*, over 100,000 victims have come forward to report their abuse by clergy in the United States alone.[8] It is estimated that more than 80 percent of victims never file a report with authorities, making it possible that almost half a million children and adolescents have fallen prey to the perversions of Catholic priests and other members of the clergy in this country. In a reversal of the overall sexual abuse statistics, boys are twice as likely as girls to be victims of clergy abuse.[9] Parents are more likely to allow their sons to go on outings with clergy without supervision, but would be suspicious if male clergy wanted to spend time alone with their daughters. In addition, historically only males were allowed to serve as altar boys, which gave the priest greater access to them. Now that girls are also mass servers, it remains to be seen if the male/female ratios changes. The Los Angeles Times has reported that approximately 10 percent of the graduates of Saint John's Seminary, the principal Catholic seminary in the western United States, since 1960 are pedophiles.[10] Father Oliver O'Grady, whose story is recounted in *Deliver Us from Evil*, abused literally hundreds of victims in his tenure as priest of several Catholic parishes throughout California. These numbers are staggering.

The impact of clergy abuse on its innocent victims is just as staggering. These survivors report significantly reduced trust in God, the Church, and the priesthood.[11] They are disillusioned, confused, and ambivalent, often questioning the very existence of God.[12] They attend church less frequently, participate less in other religious activities, and turn away from prayer and other spiritual practices. None of the participants in one study felt that the church brought them closer to God or gave them any sense of

8. Berg, *Deliver Us from Evil*.

9. Van Wormer and Berns, "Priest Sexual Abuse," 54.

10. Cited in Berg, *Deliver Us from Evil*.

11. McLaughlin, "Devastated Spirituality," 157.

12. Van Wormer and Berns, "Priest Sexual Abuse," 58, 62.

peace. Many leave the church entirely. It was found that the greatest impact was on survivors' attitudes towards God, with researchers van Wormer and Berns reporting that their research subjects developed a view of God as cruel, hostile, angry, and punishing.[13]

To be violated by clergy can feel like a violation by God, Christ, and the church.[14] For some, clergy, and particularly priests, are seen as emissaries or representatives of God in the world, preaching and teaching with divine authority and leading their congregations as exemplars of Christ. Some believe that when a Catholic priest consecrates the host (the elements of Holy Communion), he becomes one with Christ in this act. Therefore, to be sexually abused by the embodiment of the Divine on earth may certainly feel as though one is being violated by God, or at the very least that God sanctions the abuse.[15]

How then is a survivor to deal with such abuse? Catholics in the not-so-distant past were often raised to be docile followers of church teachings, or as one survivor states in *Deliver Us from Evil*, "Good Catholics are supposed to pay, pray, and obey."[16] How could obedient children resist the abuse when it seemed as though it was ordained by God? And who could they tell? Catholicism is a way of life. Church activities tend to permeate the family and social lives of its devout members. Imagine how a victim might feel as they watch their parents kneel in their pews to pray on a Sunday morning and receive the sacraments from the very priest who is abusing them.[17] Imagine what it must be like for that victim when their abuser shows up at their home for Sunday dinner, invited by parents who think he can do no wrong. Thankfully, this unquestioned trust in the parish priest is shifting, but the damage has already been done for generations of innocent children.

Catholic children often attend Catholic schools as well. While this too is changing, there was a time when the teachers were often nuns, and the parish priest had direct ties to the school. There was literally no one in this child's life that was not under the influence of their abuser. So not only were these victims being violated, their abuse taking place under a shroud

13. Ibid., 62.

14. McLaughlin, "Devastated Spirituality," 147.

15. Berg, *Deliver Us from Evil.*

16. Ibid.

17. McLaughlin, "Devastated Spirituality," 147.

of secrecy and shame, but they were also deprived of their usual source of spiritual support. To whom could they turn?

The response of the church to reports of clergy abuse has often been less than supportive of survivors. Before the scandals of recent years, most were not believed. Alternatively, abuse claims were minimized or blamed on the victim, who was then forced into secrecy.[18] Victims were often stigmatized and shunned, and perhaps even worse, portrayed as enemies of the church and prevented from receiving Holy Communion. When Communion is viewed as the sole means of salvation, the victim might easily feel that heaven is beyond their grasp. In an attempt to further their own healing, some of Father O'Grady's survivors attempted to deliver a letter about their abuse to Pope John-Paul II, but they were summarily denied admittance to the Vatican at the last minute.[19] Mormon women who experienced abuse at the hands of church leaders also reported widespread denial. Even when their reports were believed, the burden was placed on the survivors to forgive their perpetrator and move on.[20] This attitude is common in many fundamentalist Protestant churches as well. There is huge pressure to forgive and forget, and if that doesn't happen, the survivor is accused of not being a very good Christian.

One of Father O'Grady's victims was Ann, a young girl whose parents took the new Irish priest under their wing. Ann's mother was also Irish and enjoyed the company of someone with whom she could share reminiscences of the homeland. As a result, Father O'Grady was a frequent guest in their home. He was also the principal of Ann's school. The entire family idolized their priest. "He was the closest thing to God that we knew," Ann said.[21] But when he began molesting her, she felt that she had nowhere to turn. There was no part of her life in which he wasn't a prominent figure. He would often send for her during the school day and abuse her in his office as her teacher continued to instruct Ann's classmates, oblivious to what was happening in the principal's office. It was only years later, after O'Grady had been transferred several times and allegations of abuse were starting to spread, that Ann's parents asked her if he had ever touched her. When they discovered that he had, her parents were destroyed. Her father, a convert to Catholicism, felt betrayed by his adopted church and could no

---

18. Van Wormer and Berns, "Priest Sexual Abuse," 61–62.

19. Berg, *Deliver Us from Evil*.

20. Gerdes, et al., cited in van Wormer and Berns, "Priest Sexual Abuse," 55.

21. Berg, *Deliver Us from Evil*.

longer bear to attend Mass. His faith in God was shattered. Ann's faith has also been shaken, but she is seeking to regain it. Her healing is an ongoing process, but the ramifications of her abuse continue. "It's still not over," she says.[22] If one day she decides to marry in a Catholic church, her father, who has stated he would never step inside one again, would not be present at her wedding.

Kathleen, a social worker in her fifties, was raised Catholic and was highly involved in the activities of her parish. At the age of thirteen, she developed a crush on the young priest for whom she did some minor clerical work. He seemed to encourage this infatuation with long conversations and intimate hugs. He gave Kathleen the understanding and affection that she was not getting from her parents at home. This went on until he discovered that he was being transferred. The priest took Kathleen on a car ride to break the news, and when she became visibly upset, he ridiculed her for having feelings for him or for imagining that he might have feelings for her. He continued this humiliating diatribe until his young victim thought she would die of shame. Then he drove her home with his arm around her tightly, pulling her close to his body like nothing had happened. Then when they got close to her home, he pushed her away from him as though repulsed. While this priest never actually molested her, his actions were both inappropriate and abusive. This was to be only the first of Kathleen's violations by priests.

The next incident occurred four years later when she was doing youth work with a priest in his thirties. Over time, he began to single Kathleen out for long talks at his apartment. They would drink wine even though she was only seventeen and sit in the dark looking at stars in the night sky. These evening encounters gradually progressed from the priest putting his arm around her, to hugging and kissing, to stroking her back and sliding his hands under her bra. When Kathleen ultimately pushed him away, he drove her home, telling her how deluded she was about the relationship and shaming her for her interest in him. He never contacted her again.

Due to these and other factors, Kathleen left the Catholic Church and converted to another religion at the age of twenty. It was this conversion that contributed to her third incident of clergy abuse. After a family wedding, her father arranged for the priest who had performed the ceremony, his cousin, to drive Kathleen home from the reception. He hoped that the priest would use his influence to persuade his daughter to return to the

22. Ibid.

church. As they sat in the priest's car, parked in the darkened driveway, she told him that it had been a difficult choice and how hard it was for her to have her parents be so angry at her. The priest expressed his sympathy for her and told her he would like to comfort her. He suddenly leaned over and kissed her, grabbing her hand and forcing her to masturbate him. It took several minutes before Kathleen was able to extricate herself from his grasp and run into the house.

Kathleen's devout faith taught her to trust and revere the priesthood. Her relationships with them filled a void in her, and she longed to be close to them and to learn from them. When these relationships were betrayed, she felt that she was to blame, that her wickedness led her to tempt the priests and cause them to sin. She carried this shame with her for many years. And when the priests punished her with their shaming words for having loving feelings towards them, it profoundly impacted her concept of God. She came to believe that God laughs at those who are weak or make mistakes, and that God only pretends to care about God's children. She felt that God is capricious and arbitrary, making people suffer out of perverse enjoyment of God's own power. Fortunately, Kathleen was not willing to give up on her faith altogether, and through many years of therapy, prayer, spiritual reading, and a profound experience of healing in which God's presence was made manifest, she came to believe that God was not a party to the abuse that occurred and did not condone the acts of those who hurt her. She knows now that those priests were not the instruments of God and did not reflect God's true nature.

HEALING PRACTICE 5

Sometimes people make the mistake of believing that God and church are one and the same. We think that if we want to have a relationship with God, we have to be connected to a church, and vice versa. In actuality, it is important to separate God from the church. In reality, the church was a flawed human response to Christ's teachings. Jesus never intended to start a new church. Instead, he came to show humanity the true nature of God. Unfortunately, few people really understood his message. Church is an imperfect human institution. Look at the history of the church— the many doctrinal arguments, the divisions, the wars and inquisitions, and the multitude of denominations that came about because nobody could agree on anything from basic theology to what version of the Bible we should read or how often we should celebrate Communion. This doesn't mean that the church itself is bad. It's not. But it is also not God. At its best, the church can reveal the Divine and elevate our lives in significant ways. The church is capable of doing great good in the world, and is the source of some of the greatest humanitarian efforts of our time. It offers us a place of loving community and meaningful worship. Ideally, it lives into Christ's vision of the kingdom of God. But we must remember that churches are sometimes administered by flawed human beings whose lives fall far short of the example to which God calls us. And some of those people are capable of egregious sins against God's children.

- Think about your own church, or if you no longer attend, think about the church of your childhood. What are the teachings that you agree with? What are the teachings that you are confused by? Are there some articles of doctrine with which you completely disagree? Know that questioning is acceptable and healthy. Perhaps you might seek out people of faith who might help you find the answers to those questions.

- Can you consider the possibility that your church does not have the inside scoop on God? Perhaps your version of faith is just as valid as anyone else's. In a way, the number of different religions in the world is equal to its population. We all come to our own understanding of God and how to live in accordance with God's laws in our own way and in our own time.

- If you were to create a new religion, what would be its most important tenets? What would you name it? Where would you go to worship?

HEALING PRACTICE 6

Distrust of God and religious authority figures can be a major stumbling block in deepening your faith. As much as you would like to trust, your experience of abuse causes you to fear the consequences of trusting anyone with the power to hurt you. And so you hold back, your doubts preventing you from achieving the closeness to God that you desire. There are some people in the Bible who knew exactly how you feel. Read Exodus 6:2–9. Moses was bringing the Israelites a message of deliverance, but they were too afraid to listen. For generations, they had been in bondage to the Egyptians, forced into heavy labor, cruelly abused for the slightest infractions, their sons killed to keep their population from growing lest they rise up and overcome their captors. Their image of authority figures was one of men with whips and chains, men whose fists could bruise and bloody their flesh without warning, who could deny them food and drink, who could rape and murder them on a whim without fear of punishment. So when Moses came to them, a man who had been raised by the Egyptians, they were reluctant to believe his words or follow his directions. Even when God did as promised and delivered the Israelites from their miserable existence, they challenged Moses at every turn. They distrusted the God who was guiding Moses in their journey across the wilderness to the Promised Land. Time after time, they failed to believe God would provide for them. When God gave them manna to eat, Moses told them not to store up the excess. They did it anyway, because they didn't trust that there would be more the next day. The hoarded manna rotted, but sure enough, there was more for them to eat the next morning and every morning, spread across the ground like a frosty carpet, bread from heaven. It took forty years for the Hebrew people to learn to trust God and Moses, God's chosen leader. But they did learn, and you can too.

- What is the manna in your life? What has God provided you that sustains you day after day, one day at a time on your healing journey?

- Who has God sent to be a leader and guide in your life, someone who is seeking to bring you out of the bondage of your painful memories?

- Make a list of these things and/or people. Whenever you receive something that feels like nourishment from God, add it to the list. Keep your list in a special place and look at it often.

5

Am I Going to Hell? Part 1

"But if anyone causes one of these little ones who believe in me to sin, it would be better for him to have a large millstone hung around his neck and to be drowned in the depths of the sea."—MATTHEW 18:6

M any survivors of sexual abuse share a fear of being condemned to hell. They believe the abuse they suffered was proof that they are such horrible people they are deserving of severe punishment, both in this world and the next. They also believe that, no matter how much they hated what was happening to them, no matter how much they tried to avoid it, they were somehow complicit in the sexual acts that were visited upon them. This is especially true if the victim experienced any sexual arousal during episodes of abuse. They believe they should have been able to stop the abuse, and because they couldn't, they are to blame for what happened. No matter the perpetrator's age, size, power, persuasions, threats, and punishments, survivors often believe that they alone were responsible for what happened. In addition to this basic assumption of guilt, survivors are aware of the many behaviors, thoughts, and feelings they have as a direct result of sexual abuse which may be deemed by the church to be sinful. In this chapter, we will explore some of these wrongful acts (either real or perceived), and what God's response to them might be as compared to the judgments of society, church, and family.

As we proceed, it is important to approach the topic of sin very carefully. Many churches view sin as the primary human condition from which we need to be saved.[1] Sin is seen as disobedience, and those who are disobedient are often judged or made to feel guilty for their offenses against God. However, some theologians view sin as separation or estrangement from God and acknowledge that the cause of that separation may not be the fault of the one who suffers. Survivors of child sexual abuse are one example of those who are estranged from God through no fault of their own, yet feel extreme guilt due to the supposed "sins" by which they feel judged. The various types of behaviors, often labeled sin, we will be discussing originated in the deep wounding of child sexual abuse. Elaine Heath, religious author and a survivor of sexual abuse herself, speaks of "original wounds" as opposed to "original sin."[2] She relates the story of Adam and Eve as a narrative of abuse. She sees these first humans as being victims of the scheming serpent who took advantage of their innocence and naiveté. They were unaware of the danger, because they had not yet eaten of the fruit and had not experienced anything in the garden that would teach them to fear or distrust the creatures with which they shared Eden. It was the serpent who set them on the path of alienation from God and who caused them to feel shame. It was God who clothed them and followed them into the world outside of Eden, watching over them and protecting them. It was and is God who understands the source of sinful behaviors, who remembers the innocence into which such pain was inflicted by sexual predators and who stands ready to forgive without question.

One final caveat: this chapter and the next may be extremely difficult to read. They contain many painful stories of the experiences of survivors that may stir up memories of the reader's own abuse. Please take your time with these chapters, perhaps taking a break after each section to reflect on how it impacted you and then setting it aside until you feel ready to take it up again. Share your feelings about it with your therapist, spiritual director, trusted friend, or supportive family member.

Self-Harming Behaviors

As we have seen in chapter 1, there are a number of behaviors that occur in the aftermath of abuse that are reactions to the pain victims suffered or

---

1. Borg, *The Heart of Christianity*, 166–67.
2. Heath, *The Least of These*, 17–21.

their attempts to make the pain go away. Chief among these are the many forms of self-injury in which a survivor may engage. These include cutting, burning, picking at the skin and/or scabs, hair pulling, and hitting or head banging.[3] Most of us can hardly imagine purposefully causing ourselves pain, yet abuse survivors do this frequently for a variety of reasons and may continue this behavior long after the abuse has stopped. For some, self-mutilation is an outward expression of inward pain. It gives them a tangible reason to feel as much despair as they often do. For others, it gives them a sense of control. Instead of being at the mercy of their offender's will, the survivor gets to be in control of when the pain stops and starts. Sometimes, self-harm can be a silent plea for help. Other survivors may use self-induced pain to relieve tension when they are anxious or to release their anger when there is no other acceptable way to express it. Some people experience cutting or burning as a form of punishment, purification, or purging of sin. All these behaviors are actually reinforced by the fact that the brain releases small amounts of the neurotransmitter dopamine whenever there is injury to the body. Dopamine is related to pleasure and reward and makes us feel better, even if only for a short period of time.

When Terri first began therapy, her cutting behaviors increased as punishment for the fact that she was telling someone what had happened to her. Telling was absolutely forbidden by her molester. After she got home from a session, she would get out a box that held her razor blades and other implements and make shallow cuts in meticulous rows on the bottom of her feet. Nicole would often use a belt to whip herself on the back over and over again as a coping mechanism whenever she had a bad day, and Patty gained a sense of power when she ran her fingers through the flame of a match or candle. Unfortunately, all these forms of self-abuse end up serving as a replication and continuation of the violation victims experienced at the hands of their abusers. They maintain a cycle of punishment, self-revulsion, and more punishment.

This shame can be exacerbated by some in the church who view these harmful behaviors as sinful. Before beginning traditional therapy, Nicole had been talking about her abuse with a woman who volunteered at her church to companion people who were depressed or anxious or going through difficult life situations. Nicole shared with this woman about her cutting. Initially, the woman seemed understanding, but when the self-injury continued unabated, Nicole was told that she wasn't trying hard

3. Clark, with Henslin, *Cutter's Mind*, 22.

enough and that she would no longer be able to continue to receive help or even attend worship services, because she was not resisting Satan's temptations. Not surprisingly, Nicole was devastated by this harsh and uncaring judgment, and her cutting intensified.

It is important to add here that many survivors of child sexual abuse experience judgment and rejection from people both inside and outside the church. Unquestionably, survivors have often been wounded by the church. There are rigid, rule-bound people in every faith and denomination. And there are also many people in those same churches who choose to love and attempt to understand the suffering of the survivors they meet. Throughout this chapter, as we discuss some of the actions by people and individual churches who fail to practice non-judgment, acceptance, and forgiveness, I in no way intend to single out any particular church or denomination.

Christians who focus only on absolute conformity to the laws and commandments of Scripture would say that the body is a temple and anything that harms the body is a sin. Their focus is on the letter of the law, the black-and-white interpretation that eliminates love and grace from the equation. But what would God say about survivors who self-harm? Fortunately, we have the example of Christ in a biblical story about a cutter he encountered by the Sea of Galilee. This account is found in Mark 5:1–20. A man who was demon-possessed was living in the tombs near there and would rant and rave, cutting himself with stones. People must have been terrified of this man, because they had tried to restrain him, binding him with chains, but he tore the chains apart. Any reasonable person would stay far away from such a lunatic, but not Jesus. Instead, Jesus stood his ground as the man rushed toward him, and when he drew near, Jesus asked his name, thus affirming the man's humanity. Then Jesus was compassionate to this wounded soul and healed him. I believe Jesus knew what horrendous events had occurred to cause this man, Legion, to act in these frightening and hurtful ways. He knew the heart of the man and knew his behaviors did not arise out of sin but out of fear and pain. Jesus did not judge—instead, he loved, creating a safe space for healing to begin. We know this to be true, because even after the healing happened, the man longed to stay with Jesus, to be in his loving presence for longer than just an hour or a day. Jesus came to earth to exemplify for us in a flesh-and-blood way the nature of God. If this is how Christ responded to a cutter in the Bible, is it not possible that God will do the same for those abuse survivors in our midst who self-harm?

HEALING PRACTICE 1

Below is a paraphrase of the story of Legion I wrote for a client. As you read it, put yourself in the place of the main character. Imagine what it must have been like to encounter the living Christ and receive his love and mercy. Try to make space for the belief that nothing you have done could ever be so awful that you would be rejected by God.

"Jesus and the disciples went across the lake to an isolated place. When Jesus got out of the boat, a woman who was tormented by memories of severe abuse came to meet him. This woman lived in the wilderness because many people had hurt her, and she dared not trust them anymore. They did not understand her pain and fear and rage, so they condemned her and tried to contain her, but they could not. People fear what they cannot understand or control, so they were relieved when she went into the hills. There she was haunted by her dreams and her memories both day and night, and she cried out and cut herself with stones in her anguish.

"When she saw Jesus, she was frightened, and called out, 'What do you want of me?' for she believed that he would be disgusted by her and punish her as many others had. But Jesus looked upon her with love and compassion and was not afraid. And Jesus asked her, 'What is your name?'

"'My name is Legion,' she replied, 'for we are many.' (She was referring both to the way in which she had fragmented herself in order to bear the unbearable, as well as to the legions of other children who suffer abuse and grow up to be tormented by their pain.) She again begged Jesus not to punish her, because she was confused by his gentleness.

"Then Jesus touched her and healed her, casting out her memories one by one, any one of which had the power to cause such panic that a person might rush blindly into danger (like pigs jumping off a cliff.) When Jesus was done, the woman was filled with peace and knew that she had truly encountered the love of Christ. She wanted to go with him, but he asked her instead to go and tell her story, knowing there were many others in need of the love, healing, and understanding to which only she could bear witness. And so she did."

- After you have read this story, find a way of responding to the experience through journaling, art, or any way that is meaningful to you.

Masturbation

Another of the behaviors that causes guilt and shame for some survivors is masturbation. Victims of sexual abuse are sexualized far too soon and at an age when they are incapable of understanding what is happening to them. Their uncontrollable orgasms at the hands of their abusers can be a great source of confusion and shame for them, and yet victims are not able to stop the urge to experience those feelings again. Masturbation is a pleasure that they can control, unlike the times when it was their offender who wielded absolute control over their bodies. Masturbation is also often a self-soothing behavior. Like self-injury, orgasms release dopamine into the blood stream, bringing calm and a temporary relief from anxiety. Sometimes victims come from families where nurturing, appropriate love and attention were absent, and they may not have learned healthy self-soothing behaviors. Without such soothing strategies, they may turn to the only thing they know that helps them feel better. Once begun, survivors will often continue this behavior into adulthood despite their deep shame about it. Sometimes the masturbatory behavior can be used as another form of punishment when it is done aggressively or so frequently that the person experiences pain and discomfort afterward. This was another way Terri harmed herself early on in her therapy, inserting foreign objects that caused intense pain, all in an effort to punish herself for telling me about her memories.

Some religions and denominations believe that masturbation can be a normal and healthy part of a person's developing sexuality; some view it as a violation of the law of chastity, a covenant to refrain from any sexual act outside of marriage; others teach that masturbation is sinful and an abomination. They include it in the group of acts classified as sexual immorality in the Bible. However, I believe this applies to adults who clearly understand the consequences of their actions, not people who were sexually preyed upon as children and therefore have no understanding of what constitutes healthy sexuality. Through the prophets, God admonishes us to protect the innocent and helpless and tend to the wounded of body and soul. Survivors of child sexual abuse are certainly among those wounded ones and are deserving of understanding and compassion rather than judgment. I do not believe that masturbation which arose from being sexually abused can be considered a sin. Instead, I hope that survivors can come to view God as one who has compassion and longs for the healing of their sexuality. Perhaps then they can judge themselves less harshly.

Initiation of Sexual Contact

Terri's younger sister was born when she was six years old. Two years later, Terri began to worry that her stepfather would begin molesting her little sister as well. She became very vigilant and watchful, observing her abuser's actions for any of the familiar signs. If he even started to go upstairs where her sister was napping, Terri would immediately go to him and initiate sexual contact, thus satisfying his compulsion before he had an opportunity to molest the sleeping child. This is only one example of the many compelling reasons that a sexual abuse victim might have for initiating an incident of abuse. As we have seen, victims learn to read their abuser's signals and body language as well as other events that occur around them in order to assess danger and prevent even worse abuse. Sometimes, they have just come to know what is expected of them, and have learned that the sooner they get it over with, the better. Ignoring subtle cues regarding expected sexual behavior can often cause the abuser to be even more brutal. Other victims are given powerful incentives to ensure their cooperation. Joe, the young man mentioned in chapter 1, was given cocaine by his grandfather. Not knowing what it was, he quickly became addicted, only to discover that the price for his supply of the drug was to submit to repeated anal sex. At times, when his need for the cocaine high was too strong, he would initiate sexual activity in order to get a fix. Unfortunately, these acts of protection, self-preservation, or compulsion are remembered with great shame by survivors. Despite their justifiable and understandable motives, they think that inducing their perpetrator to abuse them means they must have wanted it; therefore, they reason, they are responsible for what happened and deserving of punishment.

Even in the above situations, it is the abusive adult who is 100 percent responsible for *any* sexual act with a minor child, no matter who initiated it. Although it may feel to children that they are making a choice, the reality is that there was no choice at all, especially when someone in a position of power over them, someone who has already willfully caused grave pain, is threatening to harm the victim and/or his or her loved ones. I believe that God saw what was happening and understands why these victims did what they did. The God who discerns all our thoughts would know that their true desire was for the abuse to stop. Helpless to make that happen, many of them did whatever they could to lessen the damage to their bodies and souls. I do not believe they will be judged for initiating sexual activity with their offender.

Promiscuity

Perhaps even more problematic is the promiscuity that plagues the lives of many survivors of sexual abuse. As was mentioned in chapter 1, promiscuity is one possible result of repeated abuse. Annie, who was molested by her father for years, had confused love and sex to the point that she could only feel loved if a man ejaculated inside her. She believed this meant he loved her, because the man was giving her what she wanted—a baby. This state of affairs came about because her father stopped vaginal intercourse, which she had equated with love, when she began menstruating at the age of eleven. For three years, he performed only anal sex or forced her to give him oral sex. She wondered what she had done wrong and why he had stopped loving her.

In the meantime, she began fantasizing about having a baby, someone who would love her with no strings attached and whom she could love and protect and belong to. One day, after her father had brutalized her yet again, her frustrated physical desire and her longing for a child came together in a seductive act of desperation. Surprised by her initiation of vaginal sex, her abuser chose to do what she wanted. At the moment of climax, Annie felt almost euphoric, believing that she was loved once again and had been given her heart's desire. The euphoria lasted for only a moment however, as her father, infuriated by having been "tricked" by her, called her a "filthy whore" and forced her to douche to neutralize the sperm, thus preventing a pregnancy. This set up a repeated pattern for Annie of seduction and fulfillment of desire, followed by humiliation and shame. She would subsequently try again and again with her father and, later, with the many men she dated in high school and college. She never stopped longing for a baby in the belief that becoming a mother would make her feel loved, once and for all.

Laura's father encouraged her to dress in tight-fitting clothing with low-cut necklines, telling her how beautiful and sexy she was. Since these were the only positive messages Laura received in a critical and highly conflict-ridden household, dressing seductively soon became the only way she felt a sense of worth. She didn't connect her father's daytime compliments with his molestation of her in the middle of the night. In adulthood, Laura continued to dress provocatively even though she was a member of a conservative church. Men were frequently attracted to her and pursued her. Because they made her feel beautiful and special, she would enter into a friendship with them, only to be utterly bewildered when the relationship would inevitably turn sexual. The last thing she wanted was sex, so she couldn't understand why these incidents continued to occur in her life.

These stories highlight the compulsive sexual acting out of abuse survivors. Often, this is the only way they know how to relate to men. They use their bodies to feel loved and to get what they want. The fact that their abuse began at an early age, before they understood right and wrong, makes it difficult for them to discern the inappropriateness of their behavior. Often, their parents had not given them any age-appropriate information about sexuality, so their naiveté as well as their isolation from peers prevented them from being able to compare their own experiences and behaviors to those of others. Nonetheless, for survivors who grow up in religious households, they do know that sexual activity outside of marriage is considered sinful, and they fear condemnation for actions that they feel quite unable to control.

Fortunately, we have two wonderful stories from Jesus' ministry that illustrate how God might view these survivors whose promiscuity makes them feel ashamed and worthy of condemnation. The first is the story of the woman at the well from John 4:4–26. A woman had gone to the well in the middle of the day to draw water. Customarily, the women would go earlier in the day before the heat was too stifling, but this woman wanted to avoid the others. She was an outcast because of her shameful lifestyle, and she stayed away so she wouldn't have to endure their scathing looks or silent judgment. And waiting at the well was Jesus, thirsty and tired from his travels, asking her for a drink. What followed was an astonishing conversation in which Jesus offered her living water and a taste of the kingdom of God. He seemed to know everything about her, her five husbands, her living in sin with another man, but that didn't seem to matter. Rather than the judgment she expected, she received an offer of salvation from the long-awaited Messiah!

The other story is about an adulterous woman in John 8:3–11. A woman accused of adultery is brought into the temple by some Pharisees and presented to Jesus for judgment. At first, Jesus ignores them, but they are insistent. Hoping to catch him in yet another violation of Mosaic Law, they demand an answer. His words still echo across the millennia as testimony to the power of grace. "If any one of you is without sin, let him be the first to throw a stone at her." (John 8:7b) In the stunned silence, the men drift away one by one, unable to come up with a satisfactory response and all too aware of their own sin. Soon the only two people left in the temple are the woman and Jesus. When he sees that none has condemned her, he lovingly removes the boulder of fear from her heart with his gentle dismissal, "Then neither do I condemn you. Go now and leave your life of sin" (John 8: 11). These words stand today as testimony to God's unwillingness to condemn God's children, no matter what they have done. God sees the pain at the heart of their actions and desires to love the pain away rather than punish the anguished behaviors that grew out of it.

HEALING PRACTICE 2

Part of the difficulty in this conviction survivors have of being eternally separated from and rejected by God is that there is often a chorus of voices pointing out the ways in which they are failing to abide by religious doctrine. Sometimes family members, friends, and church members, even clergy, well-meaning or otherwise, may be using Scripture passages to act as accuser and judge, attempting to convince survivors of the error of their ways. They may sincerely want the best for the survivor, but without knowing or understanding the source of the survivor's pain and subsequent behavior, they often do more harm than good.

- Read Job 13:2–12. Job's friends have been attempting to explain the multitude of tribulations that have befallen him, but when they suggest that Job himself is to blame, he has had enough of their innuendos and challenges their ability to speak for God. Job knows that only God is wise enough to judge.

- Consider the people in your life who are similar to Job's friends. Do they claim the ability to speak for God? How many of them know what has happened to you or what it did to you? If they don't, then they don't have the right to judge. Even so, is it possible that they care about you and are trying to do what they think is best for you? Their words and actions may be hurtful to you, even make you angry, but focusing on that anger distracts you from working on your own healing journey. Perhaps it is enough to realize that you do not have to listen to their admonishments and advice. Perhaps, like Job, you can turn to God and receive God's acceptance and gentle guidance.

Drugs and Alcohol

Abuse survivors sometimes turn to drugs and alcohol to numb their pain or to feel some relief from the unremitting anxiety they experience. They may be unable to relax and enjoy social occasions without the aid of "liquid courage." This may have started before they were capable of understanding what they were doing. Terri found her stepfather's liquor stash when she was nine years old. She also knew where her mother's sleeping pills were. Unaware of the dangers, she only wanted to sleep for a very long time without being awakened by her abuser's attentions. Swallowing several pills with the aid of the vile-tasting alcohol, she sank into blissful sleep. When she awoke in a pool of her own vomit, her stepfather was looming over her and proceeded to exact his sexual punishment on her for using drugs and alcohol. Despite the negative consequences of her actions, Terri learned to crave the release she had felt in those moments before she lost consciousness. Joe, who I mentioned above, was given cocaine during episodes of sexual abuse and was hooked before he even knew what this white powdery substance was. He just knew that it made him feel powerful and on top of the world. He felt in control when nothing in his life was controllable. By the time I met him, he had kicked the habit, but not before spending his college years in a cocaine-induced high.

So how does God view the addictive behaviors of these innocent victims? First of all, I believe God knows who and what are responsible for the drinking and drugging. God sees the child who still lives inside the adult body, merely seeking an end to the suffering. It is the sexual perpetrator whose behavior, over which he had full control, inflicted the original wound from which the survivor sought relief in possibly the only way he or she knew how. God knows that without this abuse, the survivor might never have begun using these substances in harmful ways. Turn back to the Scripture passage at the beginning of this chapter. Christ's powerful words to those who would cause a child to sin speak volumes about where God's sympathies lie, and they are most definitely not with the abuser.

Suicidal Thoughts and Behaviors

The frequent suicidal thoughts and occasional suicide attempts of the sex abuse survivor often lead to a deep and anguished fear of hell. The traditional view of suicide, especially within the Roman Catholic Church, is that it is an unforgivable sin. Historically, suicide victims were not allowed a Christian burial and could not be laid to rest alongside family members in the churchyard, because they had so offended God and the church by taking their own lives. Fortunately, this position has softened in recent years, but long-held beliefs and stigma die hard. Therefore it is very difficult for survivors to believe that they will not be condemned for their suicidal thoughts and behaviors. What they are seldom aware of is that their thoughts usually don't mean they want to die, only that they fervently don't want to keep living in such horrific pain. And who could blame them for that? In addition, the thoughts can be oddly comforting. Knowing that the choice of life and death is within their grasp allows survivors to feel that there is something they can control. When they are made aware of this possibility, most acknowledge the truth of it and recognize that their thoughts are only that—thoughts. They are not actions, merely symptoms of a need to find a measure of control in the chaos and pain of their lives. Usually this knowledge is enough to cause the suicidal thoughts to decrease in frequency and intensity. They can then seek healthy ways to regain a sense of control in stressful circumstances. Again, it is important to remember that God looks upon the heart and sees the pain that is at the center of these thoughts.

Actual suicide attempts do occur, but some incidents that are labeled as attempts are, in reality, self-harming episodes that unintentionally went too far. Suicide completions, while higher than in the general population, are still rare. One study in Australia documented twenty-one cases of fatal self-harm in a group of 2,759 survivors of childhood sexual abuse, a rate of three-fourths of 1 percent.[4] This is only an 18 percent higher risk than in the general population. And even in these cases, for those unfortunate few whose lives have become too unbearably painful to continue, I believe that God has compassion on their wounded souls and offers them peace and healing in eternity.

All of the behaviors mentioned in this chapter may contribute to a survivor's fear of hell. These behaviors are extremely painful and sometimes

---

4. Cutajar et al., "Suicide and fatal drug overdose," 184–87.

wreak violence against the survivor's own body and spirit. The actions are primarily directed inward, against the self. While their origin is understandable and not sinful, competent psychological and spiritual help may bring peace and healing. In the next chapter, we will explore a group of behaviors that, in addition to the inward component, are also directed outward at times and have the potential to impact others.

6

Am I Going to Hell? Part 2

"On hearing this, Jesus said to them, 'It is not the healthy who need a doctor, but the sick. I have not come to call the righteous, but sinners.'"—MARK 2:17

While the behaviors of the previous chapter dealt with ways survivors intimately harm themselves in hopes of discharging the pain and shame of sexual abuse, this next group of behaviors, while directed outward, is also self-harming and leaves survivors feeling overwhelmed with shame and a sense of being sinful and unforgivable.

Lying

I have had some of my more severely abused clients say to me, "What if I'm making this up?" This happens regardless of whether they have recently recovered repressed memories or have retained perfect recall of the abusive events over many years. This uncertainty causes them much anguish, because if they are somehow mistaken about what happened to them or misinterpreted it, then they must be lying, which is also a sin. The problem lies in the fact that sexual abuse seldom leaves a visible mark, and molesters almost always deny their involvement, so there is little or no evidence that the abuse ever took place. The perpetrators usually have repeatedly and forcefully impressed upon the victim that they are not to tell anyone about what is happening to them. In addition, dysfunctional families often prohibit their children from talking with outsiders about anything that happens within the family unit. Many survivors have had experiences of telling someone about the abuse, only to be told that they must be confused or that it just didn't happen. Throw in news stories of false memory syndrome, and you have a perfect recipe for self-doubt.

These survivors do know the truth of their abuse, but their fear is often greater than this knowledge. The anger and threats they experienced from their offender for telling gets projected onto God, leading them to fear God's terrible retribution for making supposedly false accusations. Yet, many survivors can recite in vivid detail incident after incident of horrific abuse, sometimes experiencing intense flashbacks years after it happened. Very few people are good enough actors to fake these episodes in which the body, completely outside the control of the survivor, relives the movements and sensations of their violation. Terri actually passed out in my office on a number of occasions while re-experiencing memories of fellatio in which her air supply had been cut off for a period of time. My difficulty in reviving her was enough to convince me of the authenticity of her memory. I have seen clients gagging, convulsing, shivering uncontrollably, and otherwise responding to invisible stimuli from abuse long past.

Unfortunately, rare but highly publicized cases of false memory may cause sex abuse survivors to doubt themselves. They don't know how to distinguish between the cases they read about and their own situation. If those people are making up the abuse, then maybe they are too. What is important to realize is that most often, these are cases where a gullible client was asked leading questions by an irresponsible therapist. Also, many of these cases go public because a lawsuit has been filed. Most of the survivors I know would rather crawl in a hole than invite the public spotlight by filing suit against their abuser.

Perhaps the most important question for those who fear they are lying about the abuse is this: how would God respond to the unfounded fears of sincere and honest survivors about the veracity of their recollections of abuse? In John 8:32, Jesus tells his disciples, "Then you will know the truth, and the truth will set you free." In truth there is freedom. When survivors deny the truth with their self-doubt, they enter into a prison of fear. They hinder their own healing process and damage their self-esteem with self-condemnation. A loving God who knows all things, even the truth of the survivor's abuse, would not desire these things for any of God's beloved children. God sees beyond all the words, all the insecurities, all the doubts, all the words of denial by abusers and those who want to pretend such atrocities never happened, and looks upon the hearts of those involved. Only God can see the whole of what is written there. And God will not condemn the wounded child who seeks only to be healed.

Anger

A friend and colleague who had suffered years of abuse at her stepfather's hand once told me about an incident in which she had been remembering her abuser and her breasts began to tingle. Angry at her bodily response to violations that occurred some forty years earlier, the words, "God damn it, God!" erupted from her mouth. Immediately, she froze in a state of abject fear, waiting for the proverbial lightning bolt to strike. This anger at God and the resulting fear of divine retribution are quite common among survivors of sexual abuse. To some degree, most humans tend to blame God and feel anger toward God for the painful events of life. But for sex abuse survivors, this anger is intensified by the magnitude of violation and betrayal from those they should have been able to trust. In the autobiographical book *I'm Not Supposed to Be Here*, author Rachel Reiland relates an incident that occurred while she was singing in the choir at her church. A victim of childhood abuse, Rachel was a self-avowed agnostic who nonetheless continued her involvement in the Catholic faith of her early years. This one Sunday, during a homily on pain and loss, her eyes fell upon the crucifix above the altar. Christ's eyes seemed to be staring right at her in pain and sadness. She felt a fiery rage begin to rise in her, and her bitter thoughts overwhelmed her:

> Pain? Why didn't God spare you the cup, spare you the pain of betrayal—what the hell did you ever do to deserve it? What kind of sick Father do you have, anyway? You were supposed to be His Only Son—and just look at what He let happen to you! Where the hell was He when all this went on? Is He some kind of sadist? I feel for you, Jesus, I really do. Your Father screwed me over, too. Left me hanging, an innocent little kid, to destroy me for the rest of my life. Some Father you have! I can relate.[1]

---

1. Reiland, *Not Supposed to Be Here*, 245–46.

Many survivors of sexual abuse can indeed relate to the depth of the anger expressed in this passage. Abuse, especially incest, is often perceived as something God did *to* them. In their deep need to make sense of what has happened, the all-powerful and all-knowing God must be complicit in their abuse. God either allowed it or willed it, and either way the survivor is outraged by such treachery. These thoughts and feelings are perfectly understandable. Unfortunately, church teachings against anger, especially anger directed at God, mean that the survivor is plagued by fears that their anger will lead to even greater punishment by the Divine and ultimately to an eternity spent in hell.

As beings created in God's image, I believe that anger is a divine gift, an integral part of the spectrum of human emotion. Anger can be our friend as it helps us to identify and attend to our pain. It lets us know that something is deeply wrong in our world. As a therapist, I find anger to be an essential part of the healing process. Two important books on healing and forgiveness name anger as one of the vital steps on a journey toward wholeness. Dennis, Matthew, and Sheila Fabricant Linn, authors of *Don't Forgive Too Soon*, state, "Anger at abuse and injustice is an expression of our integrity and our dignity as human beings. We must honor our anger. . . ."[2] In other words, anger is self-honoring; it tells us that, someplace deep inside, we know that we deserved better. This inner knowing is a helpful antidote to the deep shame that survivors frequently bear. And Flora Slosson Wuellner believes that anger helps to fuel an "inner vitality" that gives us strength to get through life's difficulties. [3] Anger is a physically energizing emotion, one that can be harnessed and used when people are in need of the strength to make changes in their lives and move toward a healthier future. Often, I find that a survivor's anger was what helped them make it through the atrocities they suffered.

However, survivors may have great difficulty viewing anger as their friend. Their perpetrators were often angry too and acted out in ways that caused deep pain. It is important to distinguish between the emotion of anger and acts of aggression. One can feel anger and yet choose not to act aggressively toward another human being. Anger, when channeled in positive ways, can be a force for good. Many humanitarian causes have been

---

2. Linn et al., *Don't Forgive Too Soon*, 42.

3. Wuellner, *Forgiveness*, 13.

furthered by people who got angry at the injustice they saw around them and vowed to make a change.

I believe that sometimes our anger is merely an echo of God's own anger at the wickedness of those who would choose to bring harm to innocent children. Certainly God understands the source of a survivor's anger and is big enough to receive God-directed anger without retaliating. Any glance through the book of Psalms will confirm that God hears and understands our anger. God has borne the brunt of humanity's anger since the beginning of time as believers throughout the ages have blamed God for their suffering. It is part of the eternal quest to answer the "why" of calamity and misfortune. God knows and accepts the limitations of our human understanding, all the while anticipating a time of union with us in which all knowledge will be shared and all secrets made known. And with the wisdom that comes in that union, all anger will be healed.

HEALING PRACTICE 1

In his letter to the Romans, Paul writes, "For all have sinned and fall short of the glory of God, and are justified freely by his grace through the redemption that came by Christ Jesus." (Rom 3:23–24) In other words, Christian perfection is neither possible nor expected. Sin is part of the human condition, and all of us fall short of the example Christ set for us. Yet we have all been set free from sin by the redemptive act of Christ's death on the cross. Old-time hymns talk of our sins being washed away. If you are still struggling with thoughts about how sinful you are, buy some Alka-Seltzer tablets, and write on them with a pen all the sins you believe yourself to have committed. Drop these tablets one by one in a clear glass bowl filled with water. Watch as the water dissolves away the "evidence" of all the things you believe make you deserving of hell. Allow yourself to feel the lightness and freedom that comes as your sin is washed away. Every time you start to feel stained by the abuse and its impact on you, do this again.

Inability to Forgive

Forgiveness is a particularly troubling issue for survivors of child sexual abuse. Often they are pressured by family, church acquaintances, and/or clergy to forgive the perpetrator, but this is not an easy thing to do when one has been so grievously wounded. While research shows that forgiveness can lead to higher levels of hope and self-esteem, it is no simple task and may in fact be the work of a lifetime. [45]

Jesus told his disciples that unless they forgave their brothers' sins, God would not forgive their own sins (Matt 6:15), and that the standard for forgiveness was not once or seven times, but seventy-seven times (Matt 18:22). Most sexual abuse survivors cannot manage to forgive their abusers even once. The thought of forgiving the monster who violated them is more than they can stomach. Forgiveness would seem to them like letting the abuser off the hook, telling him that it was okay for him to do what he did. Unfortunately, this puts the survivor in a frightening bind—unless they forgive, they will not be forgiven, and they believe, as we have seen, that they have much for which to be forgiven.

While this is one way to believe about forgiveness, I believe there are other perspectives to consider on the issue of forgiveness. Throughout Scripture we are admonished to forgive as our Father in heaven has forgiven us, in other words, *in the same manner* in which God forgives. And the manner in which God forgives is through the act of repentance. So in Luke 17, verse 3, Jesus says, "If your brother sins, rebuke him, and *if he repents*, forgive him" (emphasis mine). It seems like a straightforward transaction. We repent of our sins, and God forgives us. When someone hurts us, they repent, and we forgive. But what *is* repentance exactly?

The word repentance comes from a combination of two Hebrew words that mean to feel sorrow and to turn back.[6] In other words, repentance is a twofold action. The first part is to recognize and regret one's sin, to feel a true sense of guilt, and the second part is to turn away from that sinful act and form the intention not to do it again. So repentance is not a mere apology or meaningless "I'm sorry." It requires something much more. This kind of repentance is beyond the scope of the vast majority of pedophiles. Most of them are incapable of acknowledging that their abusive behavior is wrong, much less making a commitment to change. And so, in my interpretation of Jesus' words, the first part of the forgiveness transaction is up to the perpetrator. Forgiveness by us mortals would seem to be predicated by repentance.

In fact, forgiveness before the survivor is ready can short-circuit the healing process. Margaret Guenther states, "The wound of abuse is like any

4. Freidman and Enright, "Forgiveness as an intervention," 983–92.

5. Wuellner, *Forgiveness,* 13.

6. Wikipedia, "Repentance."

other deep and infected wound. If the surface is allowed to heal over too quickly, poison remains to spread sickness deep within."[7] Both of the books on forgiveness I have mentioned describe it as a process and outline specific stages that one who has been hurt needs to go through before healthy forgiveness is possible. When Jesus said we should forgive seventy-seven times, I believe he meant that in our humanness, it would take that long for us to fully forgive some of the painful wounds we suffer. Forgiveness happens not all at once but bit by infinitesimal bit, sometimes over a period of many years. As survivors name their wounds, acknowledge the impact of abuse on their lives, allow their anger and hurt, and start to heal, they may find a tiny measure of forgiveness in their hearts, and that may be all they can do for awhile. More may come with time, or it may not. But it is important to understand that forgiveness is not a one-time thing, an all-or-nothing act. Nor is it a magical erasing of all the pain suffered at the hands of the perpetrator.

It is also important to note that there are a number of other things that forgiveness is *not*. Sometimes survivors resist forgiving because they think it means they have to forget the abuse. But forgiveness is not the same as forgetting.[8] In fact, forgetting can be a very dangerous thing, because it puts one in danger of being abused again, either by the original abuser or by someone else. Many survivors have spent years in therapy uncovering repressed memories in order for healing to take place, and the thought of trying to forget it all again seems to be a monumental invalidation of what they have been through.

Nor does forgiving the offender excuse them for what they have done. As Joseph Driskill writes, "Forgiveness goes hand in hand with justice."[9] Even when forgiveness is offered, perpetrators must still be held accountable for their actions. Those consequences may come from a judicial process, by public censure, separation from family, loss of important relationships, or their own inner torment. In some cases, the survivor may never see or know if there were any consequences at all, but it is important to know that offering forgiveness, even in the silence of one's own heart, does not mean that the molester has been let off the hook. What this person did was not acceptable and never will be.

---

7. Guenther, *Holy Listening*, 138.

8. Smedes, *Forgive & Forget*, 38.

9. Driskell, "Traumatized Persons," 32.

It is also crucial to understand that forgiveness does not require reconciliation. Just because a survivor has finally gotten to a point where forgiveness is possible doesn't mean he or she must be in relationship with the abuser. Severing all ties with this person might be the only way to be safe and to continue to heal. The probability is that the offender has not been "cured" of his inappropriate desires or behaviors, and even if this person never touches his victim again, being in his presence could be extremely toxic for the survivor and severely set back the healing process.

Finally, it is helpful to distinguish between forgiveness and letting go. There may come a time when, although a survivor doesn't feel able to forgive their perpetrator, they might decide that they are tired of carrying around their anger and bitterness and want to let it go. They no longer want their lives to be defined by the abuse. They want to move past it and into a life of abundance and hope. Letting go allows them to choose not to be a victim anymore. It allows them to stop letting the abuser live rent-free inside their head so they can walk with a lighter step into the future. This act is for the survivor and the survivor alone.

Some survivors, however, may still feel a need to forgive. This is a personal choice and can be very liberating when it is made freely and not due to the influence of others. The act of forgiveness, at the right time and with a healthy understanding of what forgiveness entails, is much more a blessing for the survivor than it is a gift to the one who abused them. It can be a means of release, a doorway to freedom from the cancer of hatred and resentment that can imprison the soul of the abused.

Cult Abuse

I had been working with Bonnie, the woman with dissociative identity disorder, for some time when a menacing alter made an appearance, making vague threats of violence toward me. It was nearing Halloween, an important "festival" for those who practice Satanism. As I explored this alter more deeply, I discovered that he (females often have a number of male alters) was part of a grouping of three alters who had experienced cult abuse. The leader, known as Wizard, had been inciting one of the other "cult members" to make these threats against me, in an attempt to scare me away and keep me from getting too close. Ritual or cult abuse is rare, but its victims experience some of the most terrifying abuse imaginable. They are subjected to sexual violation in an atmosphere that is dark and ominous by perpetrators who are often robed and masked, chanting strange, sometimes unintelligible words, and surrounded by candles and occult symbols. Listening to the stories of Wizard and his two companion alters, I learned that they had been subjected to regular confinement in a box with a hinged lid. One alter, Billy, was so damaged by this that it caused great pain to straighten his legs in my office. As much as he hated the box, he hated worse what happened when he was taken out of the box. Then, he or one of the other alters would be laid on a work bench, head restrained in a vise, then abused by several men at once as they chanted their devotion to Satan. Pentagrams were painted on their bodies in blood, psychedelic drugs administered via injections, and animal sacrifices performed in their presence. They were sometimes forced to participate in these and many more unspeakable acts. Wizard was told that he was the child of the devil, and he absolutely believed it. He had been indoctrinated to believe that his "punishments" were a way to strengthen him for the time when he would continue his "father's" work.

Other survivors of cult abuse have suffered similar experiences or worse. Some satanic cults have been known to participate in human mutilation and sacrifice, which victims may be forced to witness. In addition to these organized groups, there are many individuals who are self-styled Satanists, usually young people who dabble in the occult and enjoy the sense of menace and power it gives them. Nicole fell prey to one of these disturbed individuals when she was in high school. He was an older neighbor boy who was on the lookout for someone who could be easily manipulated, and Nicole, because of her prior abuse, was vulnerable to his machinations. He would take her to his room, which was bare of furniture except for a mattress on the floor and numerous occult symbols on the walls, and molest her. Candles burned and demonic music played, lending a frightening backdrop that was often intensified by drugs he administered covertly in a soft drink. He often used the candles to drip hot wax onto her body or pass the flame across her skin, leaving painful burns. This boy had an uncanny knack of appearing silently and suddenly in Nicole's own home, which made her feel as though he had some sort of supernatural powers.

The impact of cult abuse on the spirituality of a survivor is devastating. They feel as though they were participants in the evil that was perpetrated on them, and therefore God could not possibly forgive them. They feel great guilt and shame for the acts they were forced to commit and believe they are bad to the core. They feel claimed by Satan, marked and branded by their cult abusers, and are convinced that this mark is visible to everyone. Walking into a church makes them feel intensely uncomfortable, as if they could be found out at any moment and thrown out, or worse, publicly denounced and humiliated. And if they were told, as Wizard was, that they are the offspring of the devil, they cannot even consider the redemptive power of God. They cannot imagine that God could desire to bring them into the circle of divine love and forgiveness. To these survivors, hell is not just a possibility, it is a dreaded certainty in their minds.

And yet we see in the story of Jesus and the man with evil spirits discussed in the previous chapter that Jesus was neither afraid nor revolted by the darkness that existed in this troubled soul. Jesus saw and understood the cause of his behavior and loved him enough to set him free from its demonic grip. In the same way, God can see the truth of cult abuse, who it was that chose to perpetrate those reprehensible acts, and who was the innocent victim, forced to survive in an impossible and horrifying situation. God is jealous for God's children and refuses to cede them to Satan's grasp. God is capable of erasing the mark with which survivors feel they have been branded, making clean and new those whose lives were marred by satanic abusers.

HEALING PRACTICE 4

One of the most powerful passages for survivors of sexual abuse comes to us from Paul's Letter to the Romans, in which he states:

> Who shall separate us from the love of Christ? Shall trouble or hardship or persecution or famine or nakedness or danger or sword? . . . For I am convinced that neither death nor life, neither angels nor demons, neither the present nor the future, nor any powers, neither height nor depth, nor anything else in all creation, will be able to separate us from the love of God that is in Christ Jesus our Lord. (Rom 8:35, 38–39)

What an amazing testimony to a God who refuses to allow anything to come between God and God's children! Trouble, hardship, persecution, nakedness, danger—these are words that an abuse survivor can relate to! They tell you that nothing you've experienced can possibly get in the way of God's love. Nor can your abuser, who wielded power over you, block you from the divine presence. Even when you feel far from God, in the depths of your own private hell, God is there. And for those who suffered the particular evil of cult abuse, not even those demonic individuals who tormented you can keep you from receiving God's grace and mercy. Paul says that there is nothing in all of creation, the world and all the heavens, that can exclude you from the kingdom of God. When you fear the fires of hell, make this passage your mantra. Let these words soak into your soul over and over again until you begin to believe they are true. And when you believe, allow yourself to receive that profound love and grace, for they are yours, without exception and without cost.

The Question of Hell

The Bible is full of punishment language that makes it hard for some to envision a loving, forgiving God. Some religions often spend more time talking about a God who punishes than a God who loves and longs to be reconciled to humankind. So how are we to get around all this talk of hell and eternal punishment in Scripture? First of all, many of the references to punishment are made by the psalmists who *assume* that their calamity and tribulation are a punishment from God. These are people who are trying to understand the events of their lives and mistakenly attribute their pain to an angry and punitive God. I do not believe this to be true. While I do believe that there are times when a loving God administers gentle correction and guidance on this earth, I do not and cannot believe that God is willing to condemn God's children to eternal damnation for the wrongs they do. Certainly, there are inescapable consequences for breaking God's laws, but they are not necessarily eternal ones. If we lie or cheat or steal, we alienate ourselves from others. If we covet that which we do not have, we will never be content. If we bring harm to others, we will presumably be punished by the laws of the land. The internal consequences of sin are often regret, guilt, and shame. God does not cause these things; we bring them on ourselves. In William Young's novel *The Shack*, the personification of God speaks these words to Mack, the main character: "I don't need to punish people for sin. Sin is its own punishment, devouring you from the inside."[10]

Another consideration is the possibility that Jesus often used exaggeration and metaphor to make a point. It's difficult to believe that Jesus was being literal when he suggested in Matthew 5:29 that anyone who looks at another person lustfully should gouge out the offending eye! But that

10. Young, *The Shack*, 120.

language certainly gets our attention. My husband never raised a hand to our children other than a gentle swat to their diapered rears, but there were many times when, to impress upon them the seriousness of their misbehavior, he told them, "I'm going to take you to Knuckle Junction if you don't stop that!" The effect was usually instant obedience accompanied by a giggle, but they never once actually believed their father would strike them with his fist. So when Jesus suggests that some will be cast into the eternal fire on judgment day, it is entirely possible that he was using hyperbole.

There are three things that support this idea. One is that Jesus was of Jewish descent. In the Jewish tradition, there is no hell. It is believed that people are basically good, and only do bad things out of their own pain or fear.[11] Jesus was not sent to create a hell that had not previously existed, but to provide a means by which all people could be reconciled to God. Secondly, when Jesus used the words "lake of fire," he was referring to an actual place outside of Jerusalem that was used as a city dump. This place was named Gehenna, which became the source of our word "hell." Fires burned there constantly to destroy the trash or anything that was considered unclean, even dead bodies. So it was a reference that the Israelites of biblical times would have recognized immediately. They would probably have understood it as a metaphor for what their lives might be like if they failed to heed Christ's teachings, not as future punishment, but as a consequence in the here and now of failing to live in loving and godly ways.[12] And finally, we have Christ's own words in the book of John when he is predicting his own death: "And when I am lifted up on the cross, I will draw everyone to myself" (John 12:32, NLT). There is nothing exclusionary about this statement. Jesus says "everyone." No one is left out. Not even survivors of sexual abuse. Ladislaus Boros puts it best when he says:

> No one is damned because he was born into a family in which he never experienced love and, therefore, could not also understand what the nature of God is. No one is damned because he probably turned against a God in whom he saw only a God of commandments, a terrible tyrant. No one is damned because he was despised, detested, misjudged and inwardly hurt and so revolted against everything, even against God.[13]

11. Linn et al., *Good Goats,* 47.

12. Ibid., 87.

13. Boros, "Theology of Death," 124.

(Some readers may be wondering if this statement also applies to abusers, and we will address that issue in the following chapter.)

So if hell doesn't exist as an actual afterlife destination, what is it? I believe, as Linn et al. do, that it is an inner reality or state of being.[14] It is a state of being alienated from God. And if that is so, then heaven is a state of being in loving union with God. Because God desires all of humanity to enter into that divine union, the choice of heaven or hell is up to us. God will not condemn us. We get to choose. And even if we choose the hell of alienation from God, it appears that God, through Christ, will join us there as well. After his death on the cross, Jesus descended into hell, a hell of separation from God. There, he joined the community of sinners from the beginning of time to demonstrate his absolute solidarity with them.[15] Even before the time of Christ, King David understood that God would seek him out no matter where he went. "If I go up to the heavens, you are there; if I make my bed in the depths, you are there." (Ps 139:8) God will never rest until every lost soul is brought into the light of God's love. For more information about this alternative view of heaven and hell, please refer to the list of books in the appendix.

HEALING PRACTICE 5

One of my favorite parables is the story of the lost sheep (Luke 15:4–7). In it, Jesus tells of a shepherd who loses one of his flock. Rather than being content with the remaining ninety-nine, the shepherd goes looking for his lost sheep. In the rocky hill country of Judah, one can imagine that this was no easy task. He would have had to climb the jagged stones, searching high and low for the frightened and confused animal. Jesus does not say how long it took, but it may have gotten dark and cold, and yet the shepherd continued on, perhaps ringing a bell in hopes of hearing an answering bleat, shining a lantern into every nook and cranny.

- Think of an incident in which you lost something important to you—your car keys, a meaningful piece of jewelry, money, a special memento. Remember how diligently you searched for this lost item. Did you find it? Did you quit looking at some point?

- My mother suffered from dementia in her later years, and, paranoid that someone would break in and steal her things,

14. Linn et al., *Good Goats*, 49.

15. Ibid., 33.

she would often stash them away in a multitude of hiding places. When two of her rings disappeared, rings that were promised to my sister and me, I began searching my childhood home. I looked in every closet, stuffed with a lifetime of belongings, searched every pocket and purse my mother owned, sorted through dozens of pouches of jewelry that had been stashed in dresser drawers, and combed the kitchen cupboards, all to no avail. The rings were not to be found, and I was heartbroken. The ring that would have reminded me of my mother in the years to come, sparked memories of her delight at designing and wearing it, was gone. It was extraordinarily special to me, but I eventually gave up the search. I gave up. But Jesus says that God never gives up. And when the Shepherd ultimately finds the one lost sheep, there is great rejoicing in heaven. You are worth far more to God than the ninety-nine sheep that are already in the fold. So issue forth a bleat, make a sound, call out, "Here I am! Come find me." For the good Shepherd will find you and never let you go.

7

Is My Abuser Going to Hell?

"'Surely the day is coming; it will burn like a furnace. All the arrogant and every evildoer will be stubble, and that day that is coming will set them on fire,' says the Lord Almighty. 'Not a root or a branch will be left to them. But for you who revere my name, the sun of righteousness will rise with healing in its wings. And you will go out and leap like calves released from the stall. Then you will trample down the wicked; they will be ashes under the soles of your feet on the day when I do these things,' says the Lord Almighty."
—MALACHI 4:1–3

Many survivors of sexual abuse would love to believe the prophecy quoted above will come true, but are usually quite unable to do so. They have a great desire for their abusers to suffer the punishment of hell but doubt it will actually happen. There are a number of reasons for this belief, among them their conviction that God actually sanctioned the abuse, therefore the perpetrator was allowed to commit his evil deeds and will not be condemned for it. If the abuser escaped earthly punishment, the survivor has no faith that he will be held accountable in the afterlife either. This is especially true if the offender is a person of good repute in the community or is a much-loved family member or friend. Another situation that undermines survivors' hope for eternal punishment is if the person who hurt them reportedly repented and turned to God before or at the moment of their death.

The desire for perpetrators to be sent to hell is a double-edged sword for many survivors. As we have seen in the previous chapters, survivors often believe they will go to hell themselves for their sinful behaviors. If the abusers are also in hell, their victims will be condemned to spend eternity in the same place as the people from whom they have spent a lifetime trying to escape. But if the abuser is in heaven, separated from their victim, their vile deeds will have gone unpunished. There will be no justice. This dilemma creates extreme anxiety for some and may need to be addressed with a trusted clergyperson or spiritual director.

The Need for Justice

Deep in the human psyche is the desire for justice. We all want life to be fair, for those who wrong us to be held accountable or suffer the consequences of their actions. We long for the scales to be balanced by Lady Justice. This desire is as old as Cain, who killed his brother because he felt that God had unfairly favored Abel's offering over Cain's. The psalmists echo the cry of our hearts at times with their own cries to God for vengeance: "Arise, O Lord! Deliver me, O my God! Strike all my enemies on the jaw; break the teeth of the wicked" (Ps 3:7). "If only you would slay the wicked, O God!" (Ps 139:19a) "O Daughter of Babylon, doomed to destruction, happy is he who repays you for what you have done to us—he who seizes your infants and dashes them against the rocks" (Ps 137:8–9). In modern times, our lust for vengeance is satisfied through revenge movies such as *Death Wish, Collateral Damage,* and others. And if we who have suffered only the ordinary hurts of life can nurture inside us such desire for retribution, how much more intense must these feelings be in one who has been as violated and defiled as a victim of sexual abuse?

This is particularly true when the abuser has never been caught, tried, and sentenced to prison for his acts. Brittany, a girl I treated in the aftermath of molestation by her babysitter's nephew, had to return to therapy as an adolescent because she couldn't stop thinking about this young man who had evaded the police and was escaping punishment for what he had done. In addition to her concern for other possible victims, she was deeply troubled by the unfairness that someone could hurt her so much, destroy her trust in the safety and goodness of the world, and still be at large. None of Nicole's multiple perpetrators were ever arrested or held responsible for her abuse either. She accepted this reality with resignation and held out no hope that they would ever be subject to the laws of this world or the fiery fate of the next. She wanted to believe that her abusers would suffer the ultimate punishment but couldn't imagine that God would care enough to avenge her any more than her parents had.

In the absence of any hope that offenders will face divine judgment, many survivors harbor secret revenge fantasies that sustain them when their anger and rage demand justice. A former colleague of mine once told me an elaborate fantasy in which she would occasionally indulge when thoughts of her abuse threatened to undermine her ability to function. She told me she would imagine trapping her molester in an old wooden shed, nailing his testicles to the floor, handing him a worn and rusty razor blade, then locking him in the shed and lighting it on fire. Visualizing him having to cut off his own sex organs in order to escape certain death in the fire gave her great satisfaction despite the guilt that accompanied it. Likewise, Terri often dreamed of taking a pistol and shooting into the ground of her abuser's grave. Sometimes, imaginary punishment feels better than no punishment at all.

HEALING PRACTICE 1

Do you have a revenge fantasy? How does it make you feel? Satisfied and vindicated, or guilty and unfulfilled? Do you think you are capable of carrying out the kind of violence that is often a part of such fantasies? Does the fantasy cause actual harm to anyone? The answer, from a psychological perspective, is that the only one harmed by the desire for revenge is you. An old Buddhist saying goes like this: "The desire for revenge is like drinking poison and waiting for the other person to die." The perpetrator is not harmed by your thoughts, but you yourself can be harmed by the toxicity of your ongoing resentment and rage. Your anger is understandable and acceptable, but the kind of ongoing, simmering hostility that fosters revenge fantasies can become a stumbling block on your path toward healing and wholeness. The best way for you to get revenge upon your abuser is to heal from the impact of his or her actions. You will triumph over the perpetrator when you are able to move forward—learning, growing, and overcoming the limitations the abuse placed on your ability to live fully, to trust, and to love. In the book of Romans, Paul tells us, "Do not take revenge, my friends, for it is written: 'It is mine to avenge; I will repay,' says the Lord. On the contrary: 'If your enemy is hungry, feed him; if he is thirsty, give him something to drink. In doing this, you will heap burning coals on his head.' Do not be overcome by evil, but overcome evil with good" (Rom 12:19–21).

- When you are consumed by your desire for revenge, try a different kind of fantasy, one in which you are living the life you want for yourself, free from intrusive thoughts of abuse and abuser, free from his influence on your moods and actions. Imagine the good things that seem out of reach right now and believe that you deserve them.

Abusers of Good Repute

Pedophiles come from every segment of society. They are of every race, color, religion, and socioeconomic background. Some of them operate on the fringes, in back alleys and slums. They may be alcoholic or drug addicted, in and out of jail, unemployed, dirty, ingratiating themselves with friends or relatives, flopping in a spare room somewhere, and always on the prowl for a vulnerable victim. These are the greasy-haired, wild-eyed men and women whose pictures we too often see in the papers, allowing us to reassure ourselves that our children are safe, because we would never let someone who looked like that get near them. The problem is that these people are only a small percentage of sex abusers. In fact, many perpetrators are doctors, lawyers, public figures, teachers, clergy, youth leaders, successful business people, and beloved family members. They are your next door neighbor or the person who sits next to you at church. They can even be decorated war heroes, as was reported in my local newspaper recently. When a survivor's offender is someone who is venerated by all and seems above reproach, it is very difficult for him or her to believe this person could ever go to hell.

The deputy sheriff who participated in depraved sexual acts with Sheila was a friend of the family who was occasionally invited to their home for dinner. He figured prominently in family reminiscences and was always referred to by her parents as "a great guy." After Terri's grandfather died, many people in the community, who had benefited from his work as a city councilman, approached Terri on the street to pass on their condolences and talk about what a wonderful man he had been. The doctor who joined Mampta's father in abusing her was a beloved member of the community.

Nicole's family was very fond of her Uncle Bill, absolutely unaware that he was molesting her whenever they asked him to babysit. When everyone around them seems to idolize the person who is abusing them, victims start to wonder if they are mistaken in their feelings about the offender. They think maybe this individual really is a good person, and they themselves are the only one who experiences a different reality. Outnumbered by all the people who hold the perpetrator in high esteem, survivors fall back on the belief that their abuse is deserved. Punishment for the abuser is not in the cards; they are just too good, too beloved to go to hell.

This conviction is intensified when the perpetrator is a member of the clergy. A survivor cannot imagine that a person of God could ever be condemned at the final judgment. The way in which priests, pastors, and other members of the ministry are sometimes esteemed by the faithful of their churches places them above all others as an example of righteous living. Even pastors who emphasize from the pulpit that they are human like everyone else can sometimes be viewed as only slightly lower than the saints. This veneration can often lead to the kind of stunning downfalls exemplified by evangelists Jim Bakker, Jimmy Swaggart, and Ted Haggard. Blind admiration can support a holy façade which effectively hides any number of illicit behaviors, including sexual abuse. Nowhere is this perhaps more true than in the Catholic Church, where for many years, priests were viewed as representatives of Christ and therefore unquestionably holy and perfect. When clergy have been so adept at fooling their congregations and the public at large, how can a survivor of abuse hope that God is not taken in by their righteous public persona as well?

Fortunately, we have the authority of Scripture to assure us that this is not true. In Luke 12:2–3, Jesus tells a crowd of followers, "There is nothing concealed that will not be disclosed, or hidden that will not be made known. What you have said in the dark will be heard in the daylight, and what you have whispered in the ear in the inner rooms will be proclaimed from the roofs." Based on this passage, we can rest assured that the secret misdeeds of abusers are seen by God. The deepest darkness cannot obscure their evil acts, and even if they are never revealed to the world, God knows. God will not be fooled, nor is God swayed by a good reputation. As it is written, "Not everyone who says to me, 'Lord, Lord' will enter the kingdom of heaven, but only he who does the will of my Father who is in heaven." (Matt 7:21)

HEALING PRACTICE 2

How did you feel when you read Jesus' words that all things that were once hidden will ultimately be revealed? It's a mixed bag, isn't it? On the one hand, you want people, and especially God, to know what your perpetrator has done. On the other hand, you fear what might happen if others, including God, knew your deepest, darkest secrets, even the sexual arousal you may have experienced when your abuser was molesting you. There is a big difference, however, between that which the offender keeps hidden and that which you keep hidden. He or she is hiding one of the vilest acts one human can commit against another; you are hiding the shame that you bear because of what was done to you at a time when you were helpless and unable to protect yourself.

Secrecy may feel like a protective barrier against judgment from God or others, but the reality is that abuse thrives on secrecy. Abuse relies on the darkness to stay hidden. It relies on the silence of victims in order to be perpetuated. There comes a time to end the secrecy, even if it is only in the depths of your own heart, in order to free you from the prison of silence where shame and fear grow and thrive. Even though God sees into every heart and knows your every thought, the act of choosing to reveal these things to the Divine and trust in Holy Love is incredibly freeing. It releases the abuser's hold on you and places you in the hands of God, where you can be forgiven, loved, and healed. This may not be something that happens all at once, but little by little, over a period of weeks or months, as the Spirit moves you.

- Try writing a letter to God in which you reveal just one of the secrets that you hold in darkness. Pay attention to how it feels to expose that secret to the divine light. Then burn, shred, or otherwise destroy your letter, understanding that you needn't hold onto it any longer.

Conversion Experiences and Deathbed Repentances

One client, as she struggled with the idea of eternal punishment, told me that family members who gathered at her perpetrator's deathbed witnessed him asking Jesus Christ into his heart only moments before he perished. They were, of course, delighted that he had been "saved," and talked about this miracle for a long time afterward. My client, however, was not so joyful. While she was relieved that her tormentor was now dead, she was crushed by the belief that his last-minute conversion had snatched him from the jaws of hell and that he would now never know punishment for what he had done to her.

In denominations where being "born again" is viewed as the ultimate goal of religious life, these kind of conversions are highly valued. Great stock is taken in being saved, and these conversions often take place in a public arena, such as the regular Sunday altar call or a crusade that brings hundreds or thousands of worshippers together to hear a visiting evangelist. Many who were raised in fundamentalist churches speak of the subtle pressure brought to bear on anyone who has not yet given their life to Christ. Abusers in this environment are experts at creating a façade of goodness. They know how important it is to fit in, to act in socially acceptable ways, to meet the expectations of their communities and their families. Perpetrators of sexual abuse are skilled at compartmentalizing the abuse and keeping it so well hidden that no hint of their illicit activity ever bleeds over into their public lives. Knowing this, it is not hard to imagine how an offender might bow to the pressure of church or family and enact a public conversion experience in order to impress, placate, or otherwise divert people from the truth about who they are. They might even believe in the authenticity of the experience themselves. But God looks upon the heart and knows whether a person's words of surrender are genuine or not.

Unless it occurs on the deathbed, a person who has had a genuine conversion experience should be repenting of their old lifestyle and making amends with those whom he or she has hurt. If an abuser has had a true religious transformation, it only makes sense that the abuse would stop. He or she should be coming to their victims and expressing deep remorse, resolving never to let it happen again. If these things don't happen, it is difficult to imagine that the person experienced a true conversion. Survivors can trust that God knows the truth and will not be deceived by pious words.

But what about the deathbed experience? How can one know if one's perpetrator narrowly escaped the metaphorical gallows by repenting at the moment of death? The simple answer is that we cannot, but the God who is the source of all truth can. Mere mortals, in fact, may never know, but we can consider what we do know about human nature. Most, if not all, of us have experienced a time in our lives when we were frightened, in pain, or otherwise pleading to be saved from an anguishing situation. And most of us, in our time of deep desperation, have made a bargain with God. We have prayed, "God, if you will just get me out of this, I promise to devote myself to you, be a better person," or words like it. Fortunately, the Beloved does not hold us to these promises, for in our human weakness we break them again and again. And why does God forgive us for these broken promises? Because the Divine knows that when we are hurt and frightened, we are not in that moment truly free to choose. Repentance born of fear and desperation is seldom either carefully considered or genuine. Decisions made in life-or-death situations are rash responses to a dire circumstance. It is easy to imagine, then, that a sexual predator, facing certain death, knowing what he has done and fearing the eternal consequences, might clutch at a lifeline offered by a family member speaking of salvation. They might say the words, not having any concept of what they really mean nor feeling any genuine repentance. But for God, the heart speaks louder than the voice, and God will know if this person truly desires to enter into divine relationship or is merely paying lip service to buy a cheap ticket into heaven.

God's Response to Abuse

Throughout Scripture, from the prophets to the words of Jesus, one of the predominant themes is God's deep sadness and anger at the ways in which humans hurt one another. God continually calls us to forsake our evil ways, to return to love, to hold up the downtrodden and the oppressed, and to care for the helpless and outcast among us. Jesus demonstrates several times in the Gospels his love for children and issues a warning to any who would cause harm to them. These passages give support to the idea that God's anger burns fiercely against those who would sexually violate innocent, helpless children. Survivors might ask, if this is true, then why did God not intervene, which is a question that will be explored in-depth in chapter 9. Our focus now is on whether God does, in fact, punish abusers in this life or the next.

The reality is that we do not know—in fact, may never know. Isaiah 55:8 reminds us that "... 'my thoughts are not your thoughts, and neither are your ways my ways,' declares the Lord." Kathleen Norris explains further: "Evil acts daily oppress this world we call home, but we do not know enough to say that another is irredeemable, condemned, destined for damnation. That judgment is reserved for God."[1] Anything else would limit God's judgment and grace to our own understanding. In William Young's groundbreaking novel, *The Shack*, the main character, Mack, is flummoxed by the

---

1. Norris, *Amazing Grace*, 168.

manifestation of God as a portly black woman who claims to be "especially fond" of everyone. In this excerpt, Mack attempts to make sense of it all:

> "You seem to be especially fond of a lot of people," Mack observed with a suspicious look. "Are there any who you are *not* especially fond of?"
>
> She lifted her head and rolled her eyes as if she were mentally going through the catalog of every being ever created. "Nope, I haven't been able to find any. Guess that's jes' the way I is."
>
> Mack was interested. "Do you ever get mad at any of them?"
>
> "Sho 'nuff! What parent doesn't? There is a lot to be mad about in the mess my kids have made and in the mess they're in. I don't like a lot of choices they make, but that anger—especially for me—is an expression of love all the same. I love the ones I am angry with just as much as those I'm not."[2]

Young is illustrating a basic truth, which is that God loves all God's children. Not just some, not just the "good" ones or the pretty ones or the smart ones, but all created beings. All of humanity was made by God, belongs to God, and is loved by God. Those who are parents will understand the truth in this passage. We love all our children, even those who turn away from our teachings about right and wrong and bring us anguish and heartache. Time and time again, we see in the news parents of drug addicts, thieves, and murderers tearfully declaring their love and support for their child, despite the pain that child has brought on the family as well as the victims of their actions. If these parents, who are often not paragons of virtue themselves, can love so fiercely, overcoming the most hurtful actions, how much more will the Beloved continue to love those who sin against God and humans? God grieves for all lost souls, both the abuser and the abused.

No doubt these words are difficult to hear for those who long for their abuse to be avenged through the agony of hell. It is a bitter pill to consider that God loves the perpetrators of abuse. John Wesley, founder of Methodism, is quoted as saying, "There are few matters more repugnant to reasonable people than the grace of God."[3] The desire for fairness dictates that, in the final analysis, survivors should be given preferential treatment over their abusers. Yet the kingdom of heaven is offered to all. That is the nature of grace—all are loved, all are chosen, and all have the same offer of

---

2. Young, *The Shack*, 118–19.

3. Wesley, in DeLong, "Clergy Covenant," 3.

forgiveness. Even those who commit sexual abuse. They, too, are children of God and were once innocent and blameless. And even as we know all are chosen, we also know that everyone sins and falls short of the glory of God. Forgiveness is offered as a way back to God for those who desire reconciliation.

HEALING PRACTICE 3

On the night before he was crucified, Jesus said to his disciples, "You did not choose me, but I chose you." (John 15:16) What does it mean to you to be chosen by God, to consider that all are chosen by God? As humans, being chosen has many different meanings. When we were children, we may have been chosen by the teacher to answer a question we actually knew the answer to, offering us an opportunity to shine. We stood anxiously on the playground, waiting to be chosen by the team captain for a game of softball, accepting that we wouldn't be chosen first, but hoping not to be chosen last. In adulthood, we hope to be chosen for the job we want or by the man or woman we hope to spend our lives with. The act of being chosen automatically puts us above others, and not being chosen, or being chosen last, puts us below others. It is not like this in the kingdom of God. We are neither above nor below another, but each special and unique. We are chosen, not based on ability or intelligence or obedience, but because we were each created and loved by God from the beginning. We are singled out personally and called to join the party. Rather than sending out a blanket e-mail invitation by clicking on "Select All," God goes carefully through the entire address book of the universe, and at each name, God smiles and says, "Yes, I want that person to be there." We each receive a personalized invitation to the kingdom of God, because we are loved and cherished.

- Even though it may bother you that your abuser is also chosen, let's focus on the good news for you. Imagine that you have received an invitation from God to attend a heavenly banquet. It is personally addressed to you in beautiful, flowing handwriting and sealed with the image of a dove. The invitation is made of the finest linen paper. What might this invitation say? One possibility is, "Dear _____, the honor of your presence is requested at a banquet created especially for you. You are a cherished member of the kingdom of God, and as such, deserve to be present at my table." Maybe you can write this down, including the reasons your presence is desired. Savor the feeling of being wanted and included, know

that you belong to the family of God. How will you respond
to the invitation?

However, forgiveness and reconciliation do not mean that correction
is not administered. Loving parents still provide consequences for their
children's misbehaviors, even if they have already forgiven them. They
know that children learn best when they are held accountable for their actions. They also know that corporal punishment teaches only that violence
is an acceptable response to anger and that it is ineffective in the long run.
Consequences are intended to guide the child into right action rather than
to punish. So it is with divine correction as well. The Greek word that is
translated as punishment in the Bible is *kolasis*, which refers to the pruning
of trees to make them grow better.[4] Thus, God does not hack at the roots
of the tree, destroying it in anger, but prunes some of the branches in order
that the tree might become more fruitful. The problem is that this pruning
is not always visible to outside observers, nor does it always work. To continue with the botanical metaphor, some trees are too infested with disease
or destructive insects to be saved by the pruning process. I believe in these
cases that God watches in deep sadness as these "trees" self-destruct from
the inside out and spread their disease to others.

We cannot know what kind of consequences an abuser experiences as
a result of perpetrating sexual abuse. We cannot know the inner torment
that drives them to commit such soul-deadening atrocities against another
human being. And we cannot know how this "disease" was transmitted to
them or by whom, what transformed them from innocent children themselves into someone so damaged that they would violate a helpless child.
But we do know that no one who lives behind such a tightly defended
façade, who performs such hate-filled and desperate acts, can ever truly
experience emotional intimacy with another human being. They cannot
possibly give or receive love. They are ultimately lost and alone, even when
surrounded by people who admire and respect them. If hell is indeed a state
of being separated from God, then perpetrators of sexual abuse are already
in hell. They are truly "dead men walking." Barring genuine repentance and
reconciliation, the separation continues even after death.

However, in the same way that God longs for a survivor's healing, I
believe God longs for the healing of the abuser as well. Since God's ways
and timing are mysterious and beyond our grasp, we do not know when
or in what ways this healing might take place. While many believe that the

4. Barclay, cited in Linn et al., *Good Goats*, 86.

moments just before death are our last opportunity to repent and turn to God, there is no actual biblical support for this idea.[5] Since there is no evidence that the Divine limits his healing power to a person's earthly lifetime, there exists the possibility that even after death God reaches out to tortured souls, offering healing and redemption. After Jesus' death on the cross, the Bible tells us that he descended into the darkness of death, forever erasing any boundary, any barrier that might block the arm of God from reaching out to souls in need of the redemptive power of Christ.

But what of scriptural passages that do speak of eternal punishment? Some scholars note that the vast majority of these passages occur in the Gospel of Matthew and are not repeated in other gospel accounts.[6] While the Bible is divinely inspired, it was still penned by humans with human failings. Some Biblical scholars suggest that Matthew had a particular beef with the Pharisees who had persecuted Jewish followers of Christ and sought to bar them from worshipping in the temple. So it appears that even one of the apostles was not impervious to the desire for revenge. Yet this is not consistent with Christ's pervasive message of love and mercy, the standard by which all difficult Scripture passages must be measured.

Let's look for a moment at the word "eternal." Eternal is the English translation of a Greek word, *aion*. This refers to a specific period of time with a beginning and an end, which suggests that it does not mean the same as "forever." *Aion* also has another meaning which refers to a "particular intensity of experience that transcends time."[7] In other words, eternal punishment can refer to the intensity of pain that we feel in the here and now when we are living apart from God. Thus, heaven and hell, eternal life and eternal punishment, belong to a realm that overlaps with our present existence beyond our human understanding of time, and speak about a quality of life lived right now in connection to or separation from God.

So if, as we discussed in the previous chapter, there is not an actual place that we conceive of as hell, and the open-ended possibility of healing exists for abusers, what then of survivors who fear spending eternity in the same place as their abusers? Perhaps the story of Lazarus, the poor beggar, offers some insight. Jesus tells this parable in Luke 16:19–31. It is, in essence, a morality tale, a warning against the sin of pride and the consequences of ignoring God's commandment to care for the hungry, the sick,

5. Deak, *Apokatastasis*, 301–2.

6. Wink, *Engaging the Powers*, 135.

7. Bell, *Love Wins*, 57–58.

and the helpless of society. As the story goes, Lazarus is a homeless beggar, stricken with a disease that causes sores all over his body and has stripped him of his ability to walk. Someone has placed him at the gate of a rich and powerful man, possibly in hopes that he will be taken in and cared for, or possibly just to move him to a place where that particular someone won't have to look at him and feel guilty anymore. But the wealthy man simply walks by Lazarus every day, ignoring his pain and his hunger, while he himself enjoys the comfort of a palatial home where he eats the finest foods, clothes himself in purple robes, and sleeps on soft cushions with silken sheets. But then they both die, and Lazarus is transported to heaven by the angels, while the rich man is condemned to the torment of hell (another example of Jesus' use of hyperbole to make an important point). He looks up and sees God with Lazarus at his side. He cries out and asks God to send Lazarus to him with some water. He clearly desires to maintain the earthly pecking order. (It is interesting to note that, even in this proverbial hell, the man is able to converse with God, suggestive of God's ongoing efforts to save us even after death.) But God refuses to make Lazarus serve the man who had abandoned him in life, saying "between us and you a great chasm has been fixed" (Luke 15:26a).

Two things are especially important to me about this passage. One is that in the kingdom of God, there is a radical reversal of power. As Jesus says, "so the last will be first, and the first will be last" (Matt 20:16). Those who were rich and powerful on earth will no longer be higher than anyone else. For survivors of abuse, this means that their offender will no longer have any power over them whatsoever. Secondly, I believe that the "great chasm" means that God will provide separation for the survivor from his or her abuser if that is what is needed for healing to take place. Heaven is not a state of fear, but a state of ultimate healing and peace. Not only will the survivor be healed, but the abuser can be as well. And in the fullness of God's time, there may be reconciliation, but until that time, I believe that God will preserve the necessary distance between the two.

HEALING PRACTICE 4

As a survivor of abuse, it is probably difficult to imagine a safe place where your abuser cannot reach you or continue to intimidate and frighten you. Think for a moment about that "great chasm" that the Bible tells us will be fixed between us and those who would cause us harm.

- How great a chasm would it need to be in order for you to feel safe? Is the Grand Canyon big enough? The Pacific Ocean? And what if God placed all the angels of heaven in the gap to protect you from the one who molested you?

- Read some of the descriptions of angels in the book of Revelation. They are sometimes fearsome creatures with eyes of fire and swords springing forth from their mouths, much fiercer than our popular images of angels with halos and fluffy white wings.

- Create an image that conjures up this great, protective chasm and keeps you safe for all time from your abuser. Know that heaven will be such a place for you.

HEALING PRACTICE 5

One of my favorite stories about heaven and hell goes like this. A man died and found himself at the pearly gates. Saint Peter offered to give the man a tour of heaven and hell so he could make an informed choice about where he wanted to spend eternity. Hell was their first destination. The man was surprised to see a huge banquet hall with tables full of a vast array of food. Despite this abundance, the people lining the tables were emaciated, clearly malnourished, and moaning in agony. When he looked closer, the man saw that the only utensils available to these starving souls were spoons with handles two feet long, making it impossible for them to get the spoons into their mouths. Hell for these people was to spend eternity looking at a mouth-watering bounty while unable to partake in it. The man was shaken by this scene and was eager to move on to his tour of heaven. Imagine his surprise when, upon their arrival, he saw the very same banquet hall, the very same tables full of delicious food, and the same long spoons. He asked Saint Peter if they were in the right place and was assured that they were. It was only when he turned to look again that he noticed the difference. The healthy, well-fed residents of heaven were using those long spoons to feed each other.

This story speaks directly to the idea of heaven or hell as a state of mind. God generously provides the same abundance to everyone. Sadly, the residents of hell in the story were condemned by their own selfishness, and starvation was their lot. Heaven, however, was defined by the love of its occupants for one another. In sharing the banquet, each received his or her fill.

- Ponder this story for a while. If this is the definition of heaven and hell, where do you think you are? Where is your abuser?

- What does it say about how you want to live your life here on earth? If you are in this heaven, does it matter if your abuser is there as well, perhaps at the far end of the table from you?

8

Will the Real God Please Stand Up?

Exploring Images of God

*"To whom, then, will you compare God? What image
will you compare him to?"—ISAIAH 40:18*

Survivors' Images of God

Quite often, the biggest block to a survivor's ability to be in relationship with God is his or her image of God. Their images of the holy tend to be stern and foreboding, even frightening. God may be viewed as a throw-the-book-at-'em judge, a father who doesn't spare the rod, a distant and uncaring king who rules with an iron fist, or a fiery deity who hurls lightning bolts without hesitation. Terri's God-image was that of a judge, one who scrutinized her every word and deed and judged her harshly for the smallest mistake. As a result, Terri lived in fear of stepping out of line. She was constantly trying to figure out what God and other people expected of her so she could please them, thus avoiding their perceived disappointment, anger, or judgment. Any negative events in her life were viewed as punishments which she must have deserved. She is certainly not alone in this. A lot of people who have *not* been abused carry this same image.

The problem is that it is such an inaccurate image. While the Bible does speak of God as judge, this is not necessarily a negative role. Let's consider the judges of today. While individually they are definitely a mixed bag, as a whole they are usually regarded as fair and wise. They also are not the ones who determine guilt or innocence; it is their role to preside over a trial with impartiality and to rule on points of law in the process. The judges of the Old Testament served a slightly different function. They were tribal elders, leaders of the nation of Israel before the time of the kings. The judges were selected for their wisdom and compassion, and they acted more as mediators, listening to disputes between their people and helping them to resolve their complaints. Judges also were warriors, leading their people into battle and protecting the land from invasion by other nations. They were a source of inspiration, security, and comfort.

But if we want to use the courtroom analogy of God as judge, let us at least be more accurate. If God is judge, then Jesus is the defense attorney, advocating for every believer with compassion and understanding. One of the names for Jesus is *parakletos*, which roughly translates to "our defense attorney who justifies us."[1] And in Revelation, it is Satan who is referred to as the "accuser of our brothers, who accuses them before our God day and night" (Rev 12:10). The word "Satan" literally translates "accuser." So in our courtroom scenario, Satan is the prosecuting attorney, the one who accuses us before the judge and works to get a guilty verdict and a severe sentence. But as Paul so beautifully writes in Romans, "If God (in the person of Christ) is for us, who can be against us?" (Rom 8:31b) With Jesus as our advocate, we will be acquitted in the courts of God every time.

However, the act of judging is not limited to this legalistic sense. In the course of human life, we judge things every day. This is not always a negative thing. In fact, judgment is an essential evaluative function, a way of processing the information that bombards us daily, distinguishing between trustworthy and untrustworthy people, healthy and unhealthy behaviors, and positive or negative situations or ideas. We need these judgments in order to determine the appropriate reaction to the people and situations we encounter on a daily basis. If we combine this definition of judgment with the concept of tribal elder, perhaps we can view God's judging role in a different light. This God, rather than one who seeks to punish, would instead be evaluating our thoughts and behaviors with love and wisdom, seeking to guide us toward a way of life that brings us into right relationship with God and others. This God would gently turn us away from wrong paths and lead us in the direction of healing and wholeness.

---

1. Linn et al., *Good Goats,* 21.

HEALING PRACTICE 1

"Moreover, the Father judges no one, but has entrusted all judgment to the Son." These are the words of Jesus as recorded in John 5:22. They seem to stand in contradiction to the many other passages in the Bible that speak of God as judge. The Bible is full of such contradictions, which makes it difficult for us to discern what to believe. If God does indeed entrust judgment to God's son, how do you think Jesus will judge? Remember his response to the woman caught in adultery. Did he condemn or forgive? Jesus' entire being is love. If your image of God has been the image of a judge, practice hearing these words: "I hereby sentence you to life—a life of abundance, love, and forgiveness."

Samantha, a woman who was molested by her stepfather, viewed God as a stern, angry, and punishing father figure. Her biological father was an alcoholic who maintained little contact with her after he divorced her mother. This contributed to her belief that God was aloof and uncaring. Abandoned by one father, abused by the other, and influenced strongly by the church's emphasis on God as Father, she couldn't break free of this painful and isolating image of God. If this was God, then she didn't want anything to do with religion. Yet she couldn't escape her sense that later incidents of date rape and sexual abuse by a boyfriend were punishment from the God she had rejected.

HEALING PRACTICE 2

The image of God as loving parent is often problematic for survivors whose parents were anything but loving. This is a difficult hurdle to get over. Centuries ago, one of the psalmists understood and offered these words: "Enfold me in your strong arms, O Blessed One. Though my father and mother may not understand me, You my Beloved, know me and love me. Teach me to be love, as You are Love."[2] He is saying that, while your earthly parents may have been deeply flawed and unable to give you the love and protection you deserved, God is the Divine Parent, offering a perfect love that is beyond human capabilities. Did you ever fantasize about having different parents, maybe even about being adopted, and longing for your real parents to return and claim you one day? In these fantasies, those parents loved you and delighted in you. You were the desire of their heart, and their longing for you

---

2. Merrill, *Psalms for Praying*, 47–48.

was just as deep as your longing for them. Try to imagine God as that kind of parent. Imagine the joy of reunion that would happen when you welcome God as your long-lost and loving parent. Immerse yourself in those feelings. Write about the experience in your journal.

Other survivors hold similar images of a God who punishes, whether the source of their abuse was a father, uncle, grandfather, or other forbidding authority figure. Kathleen, who suffered numerous incidences of clergy abuse, viewed God as a spy who lurked around every corner, watching for the slightest evidence of sin, for which God would then administer punishment. Catholic school had taught her that mortal sins would condemn her to hell and that even venial sins, if not repented and atoned for, could lead to purgatory. This indoctrination, combined with the sexual abuse by priests and physical abuse by a raging father, led her to a fear-based image of a punishing God from whom she could not escape.

Whether judge, abusive father figure, or spy, the thing all these God-images have in common is punishment. In the absence of any other explanation, the vast majority of survivors view their abuse as punishment from God for something they did wrong, even when they don't have any idea what it was they did. Abuse survivors are certainly not alone in their belief in a punishing God. These images are prevalent throughout the Old Testament, and even today there are churches who continue to warn of God's punishment. In the aftermath of the 9/11 attacks on the World Trade Center and the Pentagon, noted evangelist Jerry Falwell, founder of the Moral Majority, publicly announced his belief that the tragic events were punishment for America's increasing liberalism. When a major earthquake devastated Haiti in 2010, Pat Robertson declared they deserved it for making a "pact with the devil" in the 1800s. Westboro Baptist Church of Topeka, Kansas, routinely pickets the funerals of soldiers killed in Iraq and Afghanistan. They do so to publicize their belief that the soldiers' deaths are punishment from God for our country's tolerance of the sin of homosexuality. The harm these and many other incidents cause to grieving families perhaps highlights how unhealthy and damaging are these images of a punishing and vengeful God. It is time to introduce some images of God that are more helpful and loving, images that lead the way to healing for the survivors of abuse.

HEALING PRACTICE 3

If you are like some of the survivors mentioned in the section above whose images of God are distant and frightening, you might be having great difficulty talking to God in prayer. When another of my clients shared this problem with me, I decided to write a prayer for her, one that acknowledged her fear, doubt, and confusion about God. See how this feels to you as you read it:

Dear God, I know I haven't talked to you in a really long time, and truthfully it's more than a little bit scary. I really want to be loved by you, but it's hard for me to believe that's possible. My parents and my abuser gave me an image of you that is stern, judgmental, and punishing. Even though part of me knows that's not true, the other part tells me that you couldn't possibly be different from every other authority figure I've ever known. And that makes it so very difficult for me to trust you or let you into my life even the tiniest little bit. I feel such great shame, because I haven't lived up to my parents' expectations of me, and I think you must have those same expectations. I want to believe in the loving Father that Jesus talked about, one who accepts, understands, and forgives, but I just can't. I really understand the guy in the Bible who said, "Lord, I believe. Help my unbelief." How can I feel longing and fear at the same time? Anyway, I just wanted to let you know I'm here. I might be huddled up tight inside my protective turtle shell, but I'm here. I pray you'll find a way to reach me in here, a way to let me experience your love, so that I can feel brave enough to poke my head out just a little. Please help me learn to trust the love you do have for me, and show me a new image of you that doesn't feel so forbidding. Take me as I am. Please."

- If you find that this prayer resonates with you, try praying with it for a while. Perhaps it will help you begin to feel more comfortable talking with God.

- If it doesn't seem right, you might use it as a template for writing your own prayer, something that more accurately reflects your circumstances, thoughts, and feelings. It's important for you to know that God does not expect your prayers to be masterpieces of eloquence and spiritual thought. God doesn't care nearly as much about the words you use as the fact that you are attempting to open up the lines of communication and have a relationship with the Divine. God knows your fears already and is willing to be patient for as long as it takes for you to let God get close to you.

Seeking Healthy Images

There is no question that it is difficult for people to let go of their long-held images of God, no matter how much these images get in the way of a faith that allows them to be in loving relationship with the Divine. Human beings tend to cling tightly to the familiar, even when it hurts. But at some point, when the images become such a barrier to spiritual growth that reaching out to God feels impossible, it is time to consider something new. The difficulty is that the alternative images are endless, and it can be overwhelming to try to figure out which of them might meet the needs of soul-weary survivors. It might also be difficult to determine whether this new image is healthy or not. Perhaps the most important criteria for considering the multitude of possibilities is whether or not this image is one of love, grace, and mercy. For Christians, Jesus was and is the living, breathing personification of God. As we examine Christ's teachings and actions, it is clear that Jesus lived by the law of love. Nothing he ever did was inconsistent with love. Therefore, whatever message God speaks to our hearts must be conveyed through an image that embodies love for us.

Then, we must open ourselves up to the myriad ways in which God might present a divine image to us. This means breaking our stereotypes wide open. Edward Hays writes, "If we desire (to see God), we will have to give our brains a bath! Our minds must be cleansed of prejudgments about what God looks like. We will have to take a brush and scrub away all those grade school pictures of God . . . . Only then can we begin to see the true picture."[3] We need to be prepared for God to show up in unpredictable forms—as a wounded deer, a homeless person, or the family pet. In fact, a lovely book entitled *Dogspell* presents an image of the author's beloved dog as a metaphor for the way God loves us unconditionally.[4] She describes how her dog is always delighted to see her, no matter how long or short a time she has been gone. Her dog, like mine, greets her at the door with such enthusiasm, it just about knocks her over. There are very few humans in our lives who are that happy to see us! And our dogs seem to know when we

3. Hays, cited in Job and Shawchuck, *Guide to Prayer*, 376.
4. Ashcroft, *Dogspell*, 15–17.

need comfort or a good snuggle or a romp outdoors to cheer us up. Dogs are with us through thick and thin, providing a loving presence when our lives seem dark and our hearts are heavy. Many survivors of sexual abuse have told me that they feel much safer and more comfortable around animals than they do with humans. Those people might like to play with this image of God as dog.

Another image that challenges traditional ideas about God is from the movie *Bruce Almighty*. In this film God is portrayed by Morgan Freeman. When he first meets Bruce, played by Jim Carrey, he shows up as a janitor, endlessly sweeping a huge room. This God is sarcastic, funny, and African American. Through the experiences he orchestrates for the title character, he gently shows Bruce that being God isn't as easy as it looks, despite all his supernatural powers. In the end, Bruce comes to understand that God's love isn't expressed through divine intervention in the daily difficulties of life, but through an ongoing presence in the midst of both good times and bad.

I have previously mentioned the image of God portrayed in William Young's novel, *The Shack*. Young creates a picture of God as a large black woman with a Southern accent, the smell of gardenia and jasmine, and a knack for cooking. This version of God lovingly nurtures the main character, Mack, cooking all his favorite foods. She slowly heals his spiritual wounds through a series of long talks in which she breaks down his preconceived notions of who God is and how she operates in the world. Her love for Mack and all her children despite their flaws and hurtful actions emanates from every page.

It is important to realize that these and every other image of God are nothing but metaphors, ways for our human minds to grasp the ungraspable. God is truly beyond our comprehension, but our need to define our world causes us to seek an image that makes the invisible visible and informs us about the nature of that which is beyond our understanding. Ultimately though, every metaphor, even the healthy ones, breaks down. Mary Ellen Ashcroft elaborates on this truth:

> Stopping to consider it, most people understand that any metaphor has helpful aspects, and others which are not so beneficial—the "is" and "is not." In other words, metaphors function to shed light on one thing by comparing it to another, but parts of the comparison break down. Although the biblical metaphor "God is my rock" tells us something about God's solid steadfastness (the "is"), we

don't assume that we can do some sort of geological sampling on God to find out whether God is basalt (the "is not").[5]

No single metaphor or image can possibly encompass all that God is, and every metaphor can contain elements that are distinctly un-Godlike. It is up to survivors to find an image that sparks their imagination and makes them feel safe, and then hold it lightly, letting go of any parts that are inconsistent with a loving and merciful God. In the following paragraphs, we will explore a number of possible images for the Divine.

HEALING PRACTICE 4

Read the following poem by Rainer Maria Rilke:

WIR DÜRFEN DICH NICHT EIGENMACHTIG MÄLEN

We must not portray you in king's robes,
you drifting mist that brought forth the morning.
Once again from the old paintboxes
we take the same gold for scepter and crown
that has disguised you through the ages.
Piously we produce our images of you
till they stand around you like a thousand walls.
And when our hearts would simply open,
our fervent hands hide you.[6]

What do you think about Rilke's idea that our images of God actually end up building walls that disguise and hide God? What are the walls that you have built around God? Can you imagine God as a mist that floats over, under, and around all the barriers we put up to keep us apart from God's love? Write down some of these thoughts in your journal.

God as Love

The prophet Isaiah writes, "'Though the mountains be shaken and the hills be removed, yet my unfailing love for you will not be shaken nor my

5. Ibid., 11.
6. Rilke, "Wir dürfen dich nicht," 50.

covenant of peace be removed' says the Lord, who has compassion on you."
(Isa 54:10) Perhaps one of the most powerful images we have of God is
not an image at all, but the concept of love in its purest form. This is not
something we can see, but it is certainly something we can relate to. God as
the personification of love arises out of our deepest yearnings to love and
be loved. There is a conviction deep inside us, a fragile hope, that there is
a love greater than we can know in our human world, a love that embraces
us as we are and sees the beauty of what we can become. All of us, to one
degree or another, have experienced the limitations of human love and the
damage that our failed attempts at loving can incur. And so we long for that
in which we instinctively believe, the love for which we dare to hope, a love
that wears the face of God. Sadly, sexual abuse twists and confuses a victim's
ideas about love. Through the abuse, survivors learn that human love is
cruel, selfish, corrupt, and conditional. It is deeply flawed, unreliable, and
too often completely unavailable. This makes the task of envisioning divine
love extremely difficult. Fortunately, there are many wonderful Scripture
passages that reveal, like a bud unfurling in spring, the beauty of God's love
for us. In Ephesians, Paul writes, "And I pray that you, being rooted and
established in love, may have power, together with all the saints, to grasp
how wide and long and high and deep is the love of Christ, and to know this
love that surpasses knowledge—that you may be filled to the measure of all
the fullness of God" (Eph 3:17b–19).

This passage points to a divine love that is abundant to overflowing,
unconditional, as accessible as the air we breathe, as constant as gravity or
the presence of the sun in the sky. The God of love accepts us absolutely
and will never reject us. Though survivors may find this a difficult concept
to grasp, perhaps the seed of faith and hope will eventually burst forth and
make room in their hearts, right alongside the pain and fear, for the warmth
and light of the indwelling, all-encompassing love of God.

HEALING PRACTICE 5

When someone has been abused, it is difficult to find an image of
God that feels accessible, loving, and comforting. It is certainly
hard to feel comfortable with God as king or judge or stern parent.
However, almost every survivor of sexual abuse that I've worked
with has had at least one adult in their life who was a source of
reliable love, someone who loved them unconditionally and gave
them acceptance, support, and comfort. This might have been a
grandparent, an aunt or uncle, an older sibling, an adult friend or

neighbor, or a teacher or other authority figure. The one thing all of these people have in common is their kindness to the victim. Whenever I have been made aware of people like this in their lives, I encourage survivors to visualize that person's face as the face of God. Linn et al. tell us that "God loves us at least as much as the person who loves us the most."[7] While the person who loves you the most is certainly not God, nonetheless, using their face to help you connect with the greater love of God is perfectly acceptable. Spend some time visualizing God with the face of someone who loves you. Imagine what this God might say to you in whatever situation or emotion you're struggling with right now. Notice how much easier it is to pray to a God who feels familiar and comforting. Use this practice as often and as long as you need to.

God as "The Force"

The classic movie *Star Wars* created a wonderful imaginary universe that serves as an allegory for the powers of light and darkness and good and evil in the world. While it has its limitations, the concept of The Force can be a helpful image of God. God can then be seen as the essence of all that is good. God is light in the midst of darkness. John the apostle frequently uses light imagery to talk about God and Jesus. "God is light; in him there is no darkness at all" (1 John 1:5b). "In him was life, and that life was the light of men. The light shines in the darkness, but the darkness shall not overcome it" (John 1:3–4). This idea of light coexisting with darkness and not being swallowed up by it can be helpful to abuse survivors. They are all too aware of evil. It is not merely a concept to them; it is a lived reality. Thus, it can be comforting to know that God as goodness and light cannot be overcome by "The Dark Side." *Star Wars* shows us that "The Force" will eventually win, but not without some extremely dark moments in the process. The Empire did come back temporarily, and the Jedi knights were forced to retreat and retrench, but good ultimately won in the end. God as "The Force" is perhaps not as personal as I perceive God to be, but an image of the Divine as goodness and light is much healthier than some of the alternatives that abuse survivors struggle with. "May the Force be with you!"

7. Linn et al., *Good Goats*, 11.

God as Comforter

On the night he was betrayed, Jesus gathered his disciples around him and prepared them for all that was about to happen. He promised that after he was gone, God would send another, the Holy Spirit, to be with them. "I will not leave you comfortless," he said (John 14:18, KJV). The Holy Spirit is perhaps the most difficult aspect of the Trinity to grasp, and yet its function as the comforter is particularly important for survivors of abuse. Comfort was usually in short supply during their troubled and painful childhoods, yet they needed it so much more than most. Comforter is one of the alternative translations of the word *paraclete*, which we discussed earlier in the chapter, referring to Christ as advocate. Another possible translation is "one who stands by you and calls you forth."[8] The Holy Spirit is indeed one who stands by God's hurting children in their suffering, who feels their pain, and who holds them in loving arms. I remember several years ago when I was going through a difficult time. My mother was suffering from Alzheimer's, my daughter was in a troubling relationship, and I was experiencing my own health issues. I broke down at work one day, and my business partner, a dear and loving friend, clasped me to her and held me while I sobbed like a baby. I felt comforted right down to the bottom of my soul. Isaiah promises, "As a mother comforts her child, so will I comfort you." (Isa 66:13a) Such comfort is a powerful healer. Receiving divine comfort can be a source of renewed strength and hope. Knowing that the Holy Spirit, who acts as a comforter for God's children, is standing by the hurting, the helpless, and the hopeless can make a significant difference in the spiritual lives of survivors.

HEALING PRACTICE 6

A comforting God is especially important for survivors of sexual abuse. If you did not receive the comfort you needed during the time you were being abused, or if you are currently in need of comfort, use your Bible's concordance to find some of the many passages that refer to God as comforter. Psalm 34:18 reads, "The Lord is close to the brokenhearted and saves those who are crushed in spirit." Try visualizing yourself as the wounded and brokenhearted child you once were, climbing up into the lap of God and being held there by loving arms as you cry your heart out on God's shoulder. It is not necessary to put a face on God, for it

---

8. Wuellner, *Forgiveness*, 44.

is the lap, the arms, and the broad shoulders that are most important. Allow yourself to receive this comfort; rest in it until you feel a sense of peace. Know that God is grieving with you over your lost childhood and the absence of comforting adults in your life.

The Compassionate One

Closely related to the Comforter is the image of Christ, the compassionate one. Certainly one of the most prominent traits of Jesus throughout the Gospels is his compassion. Wherever he traveled, Jesus was surrounded by crowds of people who were sick or disabled, troubled, downtrodden, and world-weary. Scriptures tell us many times that Jesus was moved to compassion, reaching out in love to heal the men, women, and children who clamored for a mere glimpse or touch of the Master. When his friend Lazarus died, Jesus went to be by the side of his sisters, Mary and Martha. Even though he knew that he was about to raise Lazarus from the grave, when confronted with the sisters' tears, Jesus wept with them in their sorrow.

In the early 1900s, a centuries-old icon of Jesus was uncovered in a broken-down barn adjacent to a Russian church. This icon, which came to be known as the Savior of Zvenigorod, depicts a sorrowful but serene Jesus, gazing deeply into the eyes of the viewer. Due to hundreds of years of decay, the icon was severely damaged. When Henri Nouwen first saw a print of this icon, he was struck by the way the damage created the impression that Jesus' face was injured. He wrote, "I had the distinct sense that the face of Christ appears in the midst of great chaos. A sad but still very beautiful face looks at us through the ruins of our world."[9] The cloak which Jesus wears is a vivid blue, which typically connotes humanity, God in human form. But it is the eyes of this figure that are the most striking. One can feel the deep gaze of Christ reaching into one's soul and seeing every hurt that has ever been suffered there. It is a gaze of profound sorrow, knowing, as only the Son of God can, the wounds which humans can inflict upon one another. This is an image that survivors can resonate with. The suffering savior has experienced firsthand the violence of which humanity is capable and understands the pain of every person who has ever been violated by a sex offender. In the haunting words of Isaiah:

> He was despised and rejected by men, a man of sorrow, and familiar with suffering. Like one from whom men hide their faces he

9. Nouwen, *Behold the Beauty*, 46.

was despised, and we esteemed him not. Surely he took up our in-
firmities and carried our sorrows, yet we considered him stricken
by God, smitten by him, and afflicted. But he was pierced for our
transgressions, he was crushed for our iniquities; the punishment
that brought us peace was upon him, and by his wounds we are
healed. (Isa 53:3–5)

Feminine Images of God

The church has been steeped in patriarchy for thousands of years. Certainly, the Jewish religion of Jesus' time was highly patriarchal and viewed
women as lowly and of no consequence. A God of power and might, as they
believed God to be, was utterly inconsistent with their view of womanhood.
Yet throughout the Bible, there are subtle references to the feminine nature
of God. It begins in Genesis 1:27, when the writer states, "So God created
man in his own image, in the image of God he created him; male and female he created *them* (emphasis mine)." If we were indeed created in the
image of God, male *and* female, then God must have needed the gifts and
traits of both men and women in order to fully express God's true nature.
God's feminine side is essential to the equation, and the primary way in
which the feminine divine is portrayed is in the role of mother.

Since fathers in biblical times were typically not involved in the daily
activities of child-rearing, most references to God as parent are automatically feminine in nature. The Hebrew word *rahamim* which refers to the
tender compassion of God comes from the root *rehem*, meaning womb or
uterus.[10] I believe that many survivors of sexual abuse are in great need of
these tender, mothering images to counteract the powerful male image that
was either uncaring or complicit in the abuse they suffered. Even if their
own mothers were not loving or nurturing, the concept of a God who is
all those things can be very healing. In the following paragraphs, we will
explore some of these maternal God images.

For Catholics, their veneration and worship of the Virgin Mary can be
viewed as a reclaiming of the feminine image of God. Mary is the epitome
of humility, grace, trust, and understanding.[11] She is prayed to by those in
need of comfort, compassion, and healing. She is especially seen as one
who understands suffering, having suffered deeply as her son died on the

10. Linn et al., *Good Goats*, 40.

11. Carrol, "Marian Spirituality," 368.

cross. In the book *The Secret Life of Bees* by Sue Monk Kidd, there is a scene in which Lily, a victim of physical abuse by her father, finds herself transfixed by the statue of a black Madonna and finds comfort in her tender and sorrowful eyes. This is the power of the Madonna to touch the child within us and love us with a pure and holy love.

There are numerous comparisons in Scripture to God as a nursing mother, most notably Isaiah 66:11–13 and Isaiah 49:15, which reads, "Can a mother forget the baby at her breast and have no compassion on the child she has borne? Though she may forget, I will not forget you!" The writer is suggesting that, as wonderful as a human mother's love is, God's motherlove is more compassionate, more constant and reliable than anything we could possibly imagine.[12] Anyone who has borne a child and nursed it at her breast will remember the love and tenderness that wells up at the sight of this helpless infant suckling in her arms. This love is but a shadow of what God, the nursing mother, feels for us, her children. And while we cannot possibly remember the time when we ourselves were being nursed as infants, perhaps we can imagine the sense of safety and nourishment we must have felt in our mother's arms. This image of God can be incredibly powerful for those survivors who are deeply in need of a sense of comfort, nurturing, and security.

In the book of Deuteronomy, Moses sings to his people about God's nurture and protection of Jacob in the desert: "He shielded him and cared for him . . . like an eagle that stirs up its nest and hovers over its young, that spreads its wings to catch them and carries them on its pinions" (Deut 32:10b–11). These nurturing activities of the eagle are exclusively female. There are similar passages referring to God as mother eagle in Exodus and Job. And when we sing "and God will raise you up on eagle's wings," that too is a feminine image. It is the female eagle who teaches her young to fly by placing them on her wings, soaring into the sky, then slowly dropping out from underneath them, but staying nearby to catch them if they begin to struggle or grow tired.[13] Thus, this mother eagle God not only hovers protectively over her young, she also gradually moves them towards independence while remaining a constant and reassuring presence. Survivors of sexual abuse need to know that there is a loving God who stands ready to nurture and protect them and who will gently teach them how to spread their wings while remaining nearby to catch them when they fall.

12. Mollenkott, *The Divine Feminine*, 20.

13. Ibid., 85.

During the week that would ultimately lead to his death, Jesus lamented over those who would not receive his message of grace and love: "O Jerusalem, Jerusalem . . . how often I have longed to gather your children together, as a hen gathers her chicks under her wings, but you were not willing" (Matt 23:37). Jesus longs to bring God's children into the shelter and intimacy of God's wings.[14] There is a connotation here that speaks of a tender embrace, almost like cuddling. Survivors will recognize in themselves the reluctance of Jerusalem to surrender to those gathering wings, and yet this is what they most need. The image of hens and other mother birds hovering over their young is particularly poignant. There was a small man-made lake behind my office that could be seen from my window. During one session with Terri, we were both sitting on the couch when we became aware of a rising storm. We turned to look out the window and saw a mother duck near the lakeshore gathering her ducklings under her wings. She stretched herself upward and outward to make as much room as she could for her ten or more babies and scooted each one under her wings until all were sheltered from the coming storm. Terri and I watched this scene for some moments without speaking, and then she turned to me and said, "My mother should have protected me, shouldn't she?" It was a powerful moment in which she realized that she had deserved far better than she had received, that she deserved the kind of love, nurturance, and protection that these ducklings were receiving. To have such an image of God, to imagine being sheltered under her loving wings, can be the beginning of healing. For as the psalmist says, "(She) will cover you with (her) feathers, and under (her) wings you will find refuge" (Ps 91:4a).

Images from Other Religions

While some Christians may hesitate to explore God images from other religions and cultures, I believe that it is possible to borrow from some of their ideas about God in order to expand our own concepts of the nature of God. God is bigger than all human attempts to define God, so the more images to which survivors have access, the more likely they are to find one that helps them feel connected to the Divine in a healing way. For instance, in the Hindu religion, the one supreme God is Brahma. Brahma means "that which is unnameable."[15] Because Brahma cannot be named, it can

14. Ibid., 92.

15. Thangaraj, "Christian Spirituality."

then take on all names. Because Brahma has no form, it can therefore take on all forms. This is the basis of the many manifestations of God that are present in Hindu worship. The Western world views this as polytheism, yet for most Hindus, there is only one God who has many forms and names.

One of these forms is Shakti, a male god whose divine force is used to destroy demonic powers and restore balance to the universe.[16] Assisting him is Kali, the mother goddess who is a fierce protectress. She is the goddess of energy, power, and creativity, and uses her power to release those who are entrapped by demons. These protective gods can be very attractive to survivors whose adult caregivers failed to protect them from their predators. They may appreciate the ferocity with which these gods are portrayed. They long for someone to be ferocious on their behalf. Survivors also appreciate the acknowledgement that there are demons in the world and that evil exists and walks among us, hiding in plain sight. Shakti and Kali personify the battle between good and evil and give hope for a restoration of all that has been lost. They also exemplify a way of harnessing anger to achieve a positive result.[17] They are the balance between suppressing rage and unleashing it in a destructive way. One example of this would be survivors who go on to fight for longer prison sentences for convicted sex offenders or become advocates for children who are being abused.

Another of the Hindu gods that is worth mentioning is Vishnu, who is the preserver and protector of the world.[18] As the embodiment of mercy and goodness, Vishnu never sleeps in order to keep watch over the people. He is deeply concerned with the suffering of the world, and some believe that he was incarnated as the Buddha in an attempt to eliminate all suffering. Survivors need to know that there is a god who cares about their suffering. When the ways in which some people and churches portray the Christian God prevents survivors from seeing God in this light, looking at the gods of other religions can be helpful. Using the image of Vishnu may provide them with a sense of God's empathy for human suffering and allow them to feel God's presence during dark times.

One of the ancient Egyptian goddesses was Sekhmet. Like Kali, she was also a fierce maternal protector.[19] She had the body of a woman and the head of a lion, suggestive of the ferocity of a lioness protecting her

---

16. Sanatan Society, "Hindu Gods and Goddesses."

17. Bolen, *Goddesses in Older Women*, 91.

18. Sanatan Society, "Hindu Gods and Goddesses."

19. Bolen, *Goddesses in Older Women*, 83–86.

cubs. As the goddess of both wrath and peace, Sekhmet used her power to maintain the divine order. She did not initiate conflict, but responded savagely when destructive forces threatened that order. Sekhmet was also a goddess of healing to whom the Egyptians prayed during times of grave illness. Survivors of sexual abuse are deeply in need of both protection and healing. Perhaps Sekhmet, the lioness, can be their image of divine protection, nurture, and restoration.

Kuan-Yin is revered as the Chinese goddess of compassion.[20] She is prayed to in much the same way as Roman Catholics pray to the Virgin Mary and is understood to be one who listens to the sorrows of the people. Artistic depictions of her reveal a face of profound serenity, and she is often seen to be holding the nectar of compassion which is sprinkled upon the heads of those who seek her mercy. Kuan-Yin serves as a guide and support to all who suffer and personifies the traits of kindness, gentleness, empathy, and service. This deeply caring image can be extremely attractive to survivors who long to receive just such tenderness and compassion. She can be a source of peace in the midst of the inner chaos and turmoil experienced by many.

The Jewish religion has a feminine form of God as well. Shekinah, whose name derives from the Hebrew word meaning "to dwell", is viewed as the visible presence of God in the world.[21] She is the tangible manifestation of the unseen God. While she is not named specifically in Old Testament Scripture, Jewish scholars identify several key passages where Shekinah's presence is evident. They believe that she was the burning bush that appeared to Moses as well as the columns of cloud and fire that guided the Israelites through the desert as described in Exodus 40. This guiding presence may give survivors a sense of safety when they are struggling with a lack of direction. As mentioned in chapter 1, survivors often have difficulty with decision-making and can flounder in both their work and personal lives. In their desire to please others, it is hard for them to make choices that are healthy and congruent with who they are. While Shekinah won't necessarily appear as an actual cloud or pillar of fire to guide them, this image can help survivors know that God's presence and guidance can sometimes be quite tangible if one is mindful enough to notice.

Another image that may serve as a guide is the Inuit concept of Inukshuk. Throughout western Canada and Alaska, a hiker might see

20. Ibid., 110–11.

21. Mollenkott, *The Divine Feminine*, 36–38.

images of a human form created by piling stones upon one another. This is Inukshuk, a spirit that guides travelers along the trail. It indicates that one is on the right path and that others have traveled this way before. The Inukshuk is a reassuring presence, for to get lost in the north woods is a frightening prospect. An encounter I had with the Inukshuk on a hike in Banff, British Columbia inspired the following poem:

Guide for the Lost

Great Inukshuk beckons,

signpost in the wilderness,

guardian of the path,

keeper of the way.

His silent presence whispers,

One has walked this road before.

You are not alone.

Spirits accompany you.

God as Mystery

The client I've mentioned who had been a victim of cult abuse, imprisoned in a box for hours at a time, was understandably claustrophobic. As a child, Billy came to refer to the world outside the box as "The Big." It was a place of awe and wonder, but it was also scary. In many ways, the box was more real and more knowable than the rest of his life. While his experiences were horrifying and unbearable, he knew the rules for being in the box. He knew what to expect. The larger world was not so simple. The Big was mysterious and unpredictable, harder to define than the box that caged him or the dark barn where he was repeatedly violated. The Big was a good thing, representative of freedom and release, yet Billy approached it with apprehension. One could get lost in The Big. Maybe this is a good way to describe the image of God as mystery, an image that is actually not an image at all. We have discussed the idea that God transcends all our human efforts to describe, imagine, categorize, or define the holy. God is bigger than our minds can comprehend, just as the world was bigger than a small abused boy could fathom. I remember as a child looking up at the night sky, reveling in the brilliance and beauty of the stars, and yet when I thought about the vastness of the universe, it frightened me. Nonetheless, I spent many nights sleeping outside so that the starry sky would be the last thing I saw as I fell asleep. The stars captivated my spirit and gave me a profound sense of peace. These many years later, space exploration has given us many of the answers humankind has sought about the mysteries of the universe, but I prefer to maintain the wonder of not knowing. Everyone needs a little mystery in their life. Perhaps we all need to get lost in the mystery of God.

When Moses first encountered God in the burning bush, he wanted to know the name of this God who was calling him to lead his people out of slavery. And God's response to Moses' question, "I am who I am" (Exod 3:14a), was not exactly a helpful answer. Yet it is perhaps the closest we can get to an accurate description of God. God is. The great "I am" exists in us and among us and beyond us. God is all things and no thing. "God is," as Thomas Aquinas wrote in the thirteenth century, "more verb than noun, a God who is like the wind, invisible, yet palpable, a force that bends and shapes all that it touches. This mysterious and indefinable force is the author of all of the goodness and light and love that exists in the world, so we can trust in the beneficence of this being that we approach with awe and wonder." The dictionary defines awe as "profound and reverent dread."[22] The first time I stood at the top of Niagara Falls and witnessed its thundering waters roaring over the precipice, I was both frightened and moved by its beauty. I was overwhelmed by and attracted to its power at the same time. I almost understood the foolhardiness of all the souls who jumped into its waters and were lost. Perhaps this is the nature of awe—that we both worship and fear that which is sacred. But unlike Niagara Falls, God will catch us when we jump, when we surrender to the Holy Mystery.

HEALING PRACTICE 7

As you ponder the numerous images of God that have been presented in this chapter, notice which ones are appealing to you and which are not. What do the images you choose have in common, and in what ways do they differ? Make a list of the traits that feel most important to you in crafting your own image of the Divine. Create a collage of pictures and/or words that are representative of these traits or images. In this way, they can then be integrated into a cohesive whole that makes sense to you and helps you find your way to a deeper connection with God.

22 *Merriam-Webster Dictionary*, 67.

9

"My God, My God, Why Have You Forsaken Me?"

A Discussion on Suffering

*"He was despised and rejected by men, a man of sorrows, and familiar with suffering. Like one from whom men hide their faces he was despised, and we esteemed him not."—*ISAIAH 53:3

Why?

I stand at the precipice of this chapter with fear and trepidation. The issue of suffering has troubled humanity since the beginning of time. If God is good, why is there suffering in the world? Why is there war, hunger, disease, death? Why is evil allowed to prevail? Why are the wicked allowed to perpetrate unfathomable atrocities against the most innocent and vulnerable among us? Why are children allowed to suffer from the depredations of sexual predators? Why? This one single anguished word rings out across the centuries, a chorus of voices that haunts us all. The greatest theological minds of the ages have tried to address these questions, yet clear, straightforward answers are elusive at best. And so I wonder how it is that I dare attempt to impart some measure of understanding to survivors of child sexual abuse. Yet the question of why is the single most pervasive spiritual question posed by those who have suffered at the hands of sexual perpetrators. It is a question that deserves an answer, however inadequate that answer might be.

When seeing a therapy client who was sexually violated as a child, I always prepare myself for the inevitable questions. Why did God allow this to happen? Why didn't God stop it? Why didn't God intervene? Of all the people who failed to protect the abused child, God is often perceived to be at the top of the list. We can somewhat comprehend how it is possible for our human caregivers to fail us—through denial, ignorance, neglect, fear, or their own abuse issues—but how can a supposedly loving and omnipotent God allow this abomination to occur to one who is utterly innocent and vulnerable?

This cry is echoed in the words of the prophet Habakkuk, "How long, O Lord, must I call for help, but you do not listen? Or cry out to you, 'Violence!' but you do not save? Why do you make me look at injustice? Why do you tolerate wrong? Destruction and violence are before me" (Hab 1:2–3c). Many of the psalmists have sought answers to these same questions, including the one quoted by Jesus as he hung dying on the cross, "My God, my God, why have you forsaken me?" (Matt 27:46) Any direct answers that may be found in scripture aren't tremendously satisfactory and revolve around the mystery and incomprehensibility of God. "'For my thoughts are not your thoughts, neither are your ways my ways,' declares the Lord." (Isa 55:8) Or these words of King Solomon: "He has also set eternity in the hearts of men, yet they cannot fathom what God has done from beginning to end," (Eccl 3:11b) or "As you do not know the path of the wind or how the body is formed in a mother's womb, so you cannot understand the work of God, the Maker of all things" (Eccl 11:5). Humanity has great difficulty with such ambiguity, especially when it comes to undeserved suffering. We want concrete answers. We want to *know*, to make sense of the chaos, the pain, the absolute sense of abandonment that is experienced by victims of sexual abuse.

The problem is that we think if we only had the answers, we would feel better. We think that understanding will bring healing and a release from the pain. But the answer to the "why" question does not have that kind of power. Explanations do little to relieve the suffering of survivors. The abuse still happened, the wounds are still there, and the best answer in the world cannot change that. And if survivors become too focused on the "why" of their abuse, they can spend so much energy on it that there is little left to work on the task of healing. The Buddha is credited with this teaching: "If an arrow is sticking out of your side, don't argue about where it came from or who made it; just pull it out." How appropriate this statement is to the survivor of sexual abuse! You can bleed to death while you are debating the question! It is more important to attend to your suffering and do what is needed to set yourself on the path to healing than it is to continue to ask why. Nevertheless, the questions persist, and it is necessary to attempt some kind of answer.

But what is the *real* question? If we acknowledge that understanding suffering does not eradicate it, that explanations can't take away the pain or erase the long-term effects of incest and sexual abuse, then what is the true longing that underlies our need to understand? Perhaps the real question is not, "Why did this happen?" but, "Who is God?" and, more importantly, "Where was God when I needed him?" Hopefully, the reader will find some of the answers they seek in the following pages.

Abuse as Punishment for Sin

As has been mentioned in previous chapters, often the default explanation for abuse survivors is that suffering is punishment for sin. Especially when raised in a fundamentalist church that is steeped in the punishment language of the Old Testament, survivors can easily fall back on this understanding of the abuse and pain they bear. In order to refute this belief, it is necessary to look more closely at some of the passages that seem to support a God who punishes through suffering.

In the book of Proverbs, King Solomon has created a guide to life for his subjects, based on the wisdom which he received as a gift from God. It portrays a black and white world in which the wise, truthful, and faithful are rewarded and the foolish, deceitful, and wicked are punished. At least that is how Proverbs is often interpreted. However, I tend to see Proverbs as more of an advice column that spells out the possible *natural* consequences of certain specific behaviors. In other words, the results of telling lies or failing to care for the poor and needy or saying unkind things in anger will be predictable and will arise out of the behavior itself, not something that is administered by a punitive divine parent. For example, if someone is in the habit of lying, they are likely to twist themselves into knots that cannot be undone, and in the process, they will damage their reputation as well as their relationships. If someone fails to have compassion for the less fortunate, they will ultimately feel cold and empty inside. If a person continually spews out their anger with caustic and hurtful words, they will become alienated from their community and end up unloved and lonely. These consequences are to be expected based on specific actions. We all know and expect that our behaviors have real-life consequences. When a lifelong smoker develops emphysema or lung cancer, no one is surprised, nor do they see God's hand in it. This is Proverbs logic—A leads to B—but nowhere in the book does Solomon portray punishment that is random and capricious and unrelated to negative behavior. In *Where is God When It Hurts?*, Philip Yancey points out how ineffective that would be as a parenting technique. "It would do little good for that parent to sneak up at odd times during a day and whack the child with no explanation. Such tactics would produce a neurotic, not an obedient, child."[1] Why would God do that when it would so clearly be counterproductive to God's ultimate desire to be in loving union with all humanity?

Another place in the Bible where we find a lot of punishment language is in the books of the prophets. Prophets were those sent by God to a specific people in a particular time and place in history to warn them that if they continued their sinful ways, they would be punished. Time after time, the Israelites, who were chosen by God and in special covenant with God, had turned away from the law and were living contrary to God's will. Specifically, they were worshipping other gods, engaging in corrupt and cruel practices, and ignoring the plight of the poor and oppressed. Prophets were not, as is often believed, solely soothsayers or predictors of the future; their primary function was to show the Israelites the error of their ways and warn them of the potential consequences of breaking their covenant with God. The people were given many opportunities to turn from their selfish and wicked ways and re-enter right relationship with God. "In almost every case, the prophets also hold out the hope that God will restrain himself if Israel repents and turns back to God."[2] Again, punishment was never capricious, nor was it administered without warning, and it took place in the context of a covenant relationship that was specific to the Hebrew people in biblical times. When Jesus, as God incarnate, came to earth, his mission was to establish a new covenant with all people for all time. We will explore this new covenant in greater depth later in the chapter.

And what are we to make of the old saying, derived from passages in Exodus, Numbers, and Deuteronomy, that the sins of the fathers are

1. Yancey, *Where Is God*, 81.
2. Ibid., 80.

visited upon their children to the fourth generation? Do we really believe that God would continue to punish several generations of a family for the sins of their ancestors? As a therapist, I have often noticed the patterns of unhealthy and even abusive behavior that are passed down from one generation to another. What I have come to understand is that these behaviors are perpetuated when nothing intervenes to disrupt the patterns of narcissism, anger, and abuse. A raging and violent father creates an angry and powerless child who grows up to replicate the very abuse of which he or she was a victim. A mother who passively accepts the abuse of her husband and exposes her children to domestic violence can shape a daughter who grows up believing that abuse is her lot in life. Perhaps Kathleen Norris said it best in her book, *Amazing Grace*: "Sometimes it is possible to see, looking over four generations or so, that the sins of the forebears are indeed visited on their children. And it is not because an angry and vengeful God has decided to punish the innocent. It comes from an ancestor having chosen death over life, sowing great bitterness, and sometimes establishing patterns of destruction that endure for generations."[3]

When we turn to the New Testament, we begin to see a new story emerging. Jesus, as God incarnate, exhibits a deep sensibility for the suffering. As Philip Yancey puts it, "Jesus never gave a poor or suffering person a speech about 'accepting your lot in life,' or 'taking the medicine that God has given you.' He seemed unusually sensitive to the groans of suffering people, and set about remedying them. And he used his supernatural powers to heal, never to punish."[4] Jesus' ministry is marked by numerous stories of healing, and he spends the majority of his time with the poor, the diseased, and the outcast—in short, all the victims of a society obsessed with who belongs and who does not, who is clean and who is not, who is worthy and who is not. Jesus is not afraid to touch the lepers, to associate with tax collectors and prostitutes, and to minister to people who are bruised in body and mind by unspeakable suffering.

On more than one occasion, Jesus absolutely refutes the long-held belief that suffering is punishment for sin. One of these occurs as Jesus and his disciples were walking through the streets of Jerusalem and encountered a man who had been blind since birth (John 9:1–41). The disciples, struggling with their own questions about suffering, asked Jesus who had sinned to cause this man's blindness—himself (inconceivable, since he would have

3. Norris, *Amazing Grace*, 82.
4. Yancey, *Where Is God*, 82.

had to sin in the womb) or his parents. Jesus replied, "Neither this man nor his parents sinned; he was born blind so that God's works might be revealed in him" (John 9:3, NRSV). He then healed the blind man, thereby breaking Sabbath law and setting off a furor among the Pharisees who were looking for a way to get rid of Jesus. At the end of this passage, Jesus reaffirmed his statement that blindness is not the result of sin and points out the irony that the Pharisees *think* they can see but actually exhibit a spiritual blindness that leads to sin.

Before we move on to another example, I want to clarify Jesus' statement that the purpose of the man's blindness was to reveal God's glory. It would be easy for survivors of sexual abuse to interpret this as God purposely causing their suffering so that they might be used as an example of God's power to heal. *I do not believe that God intentionally inflicts suffering on God's children for any reason!* What I do believe is that the Divine One has the power to transform the unbearable pain of abuse and to bring love and healing into the lives of those who suffer. This is poignantly stated in a passage from *The Shack*, in which the God figure, Papa, is speaking to Mack about suffering:

> Just because I work incredible good out of unspeakable tragedies doesn't mean I orchestrate the tragedies. Don't ever assume that my using something means I caused it or that I need it to accomplish my purposes. . . . Grace doesn't depend on suffering to exist, but where there is suffering you will find grace in many facets and colors.[5]

In another example, some of Jesus' followers were telling him about a recent atrocity in which Pilate had ordered the slaughter of some Galileans as they were presenting ritual sacrifices in the temple. There was also talk about a disaster in which several people were killed in the collapse of a tower. These stories are not unlike the headlines that appear in our morning newspaper on any given day. In typical fashion, Jesus honed in on what was going through the minds of those present: "Do you think that because these Galileans suffered in this way they were worse sinners than all other Galileans? No, I tell you; but unless you repent, you will all perish as they did. Or those eighteen who were killed when the tower of Siloam fell on them—do you think that they were worse offenders than all the others living in Jerusalem? No I tell you; but unless you repent, you will all perish just as they did" (Luke 13:2–5, NRSV).

5. Young, *The Shack*, 185.

Jesus understood this tendency in human nature that we still see exhibited today, the desire to attribute blame for violence or natural disasters to the victims. For example, after Hurricane Katrina, there was much talk about the failing of the levees in New Orleans. I heard several people remark that "they" should have known better than to build a city on land that is below sea level. The same blame game happens for victims of rape and sexual assault with comments such as, "She was dressing too provocatively," or "She shouldn't have been walking alone at night in the wrong part of town," or "He could have stopped it if he wanted to." This belief that suffering is punishment for sin or stupidity or carelessness is a way in which we divorce ourselves from those who suffer, reassuring ourselves that a similar fate would not, *could* not happen to us. So Jesus wants to disabuse his followers of the idea that the people who died in those situations were somehow worse sinners than anyone else. He wants to wake people up, get them to stop feeling superior, and jolt them out of their complacency. He uses strong language to get their attention, so that they will stop judging others and pay attention to the sin in their own lives. In no way does he condemn the victims or suggest that their fate was a result of their sin.

It would be easy to focus on the implied threat of Jesus' words, but I think that when Jesus says repent or perish, he is again using hyperbole or exaggeration to make his point. If you go on to read the following passage (Luke 13:6–9), you will find a parable about mercy and second chances which softens the meaning of Jesus' earlier statement. In this passage, a landowner wants his gardener to cut down a tree that has not been bearing fruit. The gardener (Jesus) begs for leniency for the tree, promising to fertilize and water it in an attempt to bring it back to life. Even though our lives might not bear fruit at times, Jesus doesn't give up on us, but tends us gently, loving us back to life. God, through Christ, offers us grace, not punishment.

HEALING PRACTICE 1

Read some of the above-referenced passages from the Bible that talk about punishment for sin. Notice for yourself the differences between the Old Testament and the teachings of Jesus.

- How do you feel about people you know who go through sickness or hard times? Do you believe that their difficulties are a result of their sinfulness, bad luck, natural consequences of behavior, or the fact that no one's life is free of suffering?

- What do you believe is God's part in their troubles? Is God the cause, or is God a loving presence who wants to support and love them through their time of need?

- Can you begin to imagine that God did not will the abuse you suffered and instead suffers with you and longs to be a part of your healing process?

Free Will

Free will is possibly one of the most troubling theological concepts for survivors of abuse. That God allows humankind to choose evil over good and in the process wreak terrible violence on the innocents of this world can seem like callous and appalling indifference. What people often don't consider is that God doesn't *want* it that way but knows that it *must* be that way. The world we live in today is not God's design; rather, it is the world humanity has perverted for thousands of years by choosing wrong over right, hate over love, violence over peaceful coexistence. We have taken God's original creation and turned it into an ugly parody of the divine dream.

In the beginning, God dreamed of a perfect garden in which God's chosen companions could dwell in unity with the Divine, and love would be the only law. God dreamed it, and it was so. Humankind, in the form of Adam and Eve, walked in the garden, being fed by the fruits of the trees and fields, given sweet water to drink from the springs that nourished the garden, and being taught the glories of life and love in the companionship of the Holy One. In all of the garden's abundance, only one thing was forbidden to them. Perhaps God was caught off guard by their willfulness, or perhaps God knew the day would come when Adam and Eve decided that what they had was not enough and chose to defy their Creator. One bite of the forbidden fruit, and the perfect Eden wasn't perfect anymore. A chasm had been opened up between humanity and God that could not be bridged. Perhaps at that moment, Eden ceased to exist at all and became not a place but an ideal that could only be dreamed of. And God held onto that dream, renaming it the kingdom of God, and offering humankind over the millennia so many opportunities to return to it. The entire story of the Bible is of a people seeking a way back to God, and God reaching out to us with love and longing, grieving the loss of God's children and weeping over the destruction of Eden.[6]

6. Yancey, *Where Is God*, 66–67.

On that day, God discovered what every parent throughout history has learned, that you cannot force a child to love or obey you. Even if you could, would that be the kind of love you would want? William Young suggests that Jesus' response to this question would be, "To force my will on you . . . is exactly what love does not do. . . . I don't want slaves to my will; I want brothers and sisters who will share life with me."[7] God wants to be loved freely, not because we have to in order to receive the good things in life, but because we *want* to, because union with God is the greatest joy even when nothing else in our lives is going right.

But why not at least punish those who choose against God and follow a path of evil? Why not separate them from those who choose to love God and obey the law of love? The problem lies in being able to identify which is which. In Jesus' parable of the Wheat and Tares, we are given a better understanding of this difficulty (Matt 13:24–30). In this story, some slaves came to their master complaining that weeds had grown up in the fields and feared that the weeds would choke out the crop of wheat. They asked if they should pull these weeds, but their master instructed the men to leave them alone. He knew what farmers today also know—tares refer to a form of rye grass that looks very much like wheat in its early growth, so that it would be very hard for the slaves to tell the difference. The master knew that in their desire to rid the crop of weeds, they would very likely pull up a lot of wheat in the process. And later, after their growth reveals the rye grass, their roots would already have become interwoven with the roots of the wheat, and pulling them out would uproot and destroy the entire crop.[8]

The same thing holds true of humans. No one is solely bad or good, saintly or evil. We are all a mixture of both. We are both wheat and tares. Alexander Solzhenitsyn writes, "The line separating good and evil passes not through states, nor between classes, nor between political parties either—but right through every human heart—and through *all* human hearts."[9] That line runs through the hearts of sex offenders as well. Even the worst offenders have some good in them. If God pulls out every plant that might be a weed, we are all at risk. But God loves us all enough to give us a chance to grow and to discover the good that was planted in us, to choose love over hate, to choose God over selfish desire. "The Lord is not slow

<hr />

7. Young, *The Shack,* 145–46.

8. Moore, *Lamb,* 393.

9. Solzhenitsyn, cited in Yancey, *Where Is God,* 87.

about his promise, as some think of slowness, but is patient with you, not wanting any to perish, but all to come to repentance" (2 Pet 3:9).

In all of creation, humans are the only living beings that have the ability to choose. God gave us this choice. God wants to be in freely chosen relationship with us and is willing to wait for us to return to the divine embrace. To force that relationship would be an imprisonment of sorts, an abuse that defies the true nature of the Divine. Sexual abuse survivors know full well what it is like to be forced into an unwanted relationship with someone whose actions are fueled not by love but by their own selfish desires. But by allowing us to choose for or against God, God is forced to watch on in sorrow as those who choose to remain outside the realm of heaven inflict ever more suffering on a hurting world. Phillip Yancey writes, "The Bible communicates no message with more certainty than God's displeasure with the state of creation and the state of humanity. . . . That this world spoiled by evil and suffering still exists at all is an example of God's mercy, not his cruelty."[10]

God's Sorrow

Indeed, I believe that God's tears fall like rain at the pain and suffering of humanity. I remember as a child learning that the shortest verse in the Bible was "Jesus wept." (John 11:35) As I consider that now, I wonder if any other two-word sentence would have had the same impact. If the shortest verse was "Jesus prayed," or "They listened," would anyone remember it? I don't think so. The impact of that statement was that Jesus empathized so deeply with the human condition that he shed tears. It was Jesus' compassion for Mary and Martha's grief over the loss of their brother that caused him to weep. Jesus already knew he was going to raise Lazarus from the dead, so he wasn't mourning his dead friend. He was entering into the sorrow of the sisters.

And so it is with God. Numerous scriptural passages convey God's sorrow over the hurts we humans cause one another. Isaiah tells us, "In all their distress, he too was distressed," (Isa 63:9a) and, "he was appalled that there was no one to intervene" (Isa 59:15b–16a). In the book of Jeremiah, God speaks these words of sorrow: "Since my people are crushed, I am crushed; I mourn, and horror grips me" (Jer 8:21). I believe that God grieves especially over the sexual abuse of children. Many of the prophets

10. Ibid., 68.

speak to God's desire for consideration to be given to those who are in special need of protection—the innocent, the helpless, and the lowly of society. Centuries later, Jesus modeled this message in his relationships with children. In a time when children were not valued or given importance in the Hebrew culture, Jesus held them up as an example of true faith (Matt 18:2–4) and often singled them out for loving attention. He listened to them when others wanted them to be shooed away (Matt 19:13–15). There are also many examples of Jesus healing children. These stories convince me that the very thought of children being subject to incest and sexual abuse would be extraordinarily painful to him.

A contemporary hymn, "God Weeps," offers us a poignant expression of God's sorrow over a suffering humanity, especially the first verse:

> God weeps at love withheld,
> at strength misused,
> at children's innocence abused,
> and till we change the way we love,
> God weeps.[11]

And it was out of this sorrow, this desire to reach out with compassion and comfort, that God sent Jesus to become one of us, to bridge the chasm that had divided humankind from their Creator since Eden, to show us firsthand the love God has for each of us and how we are to love one another.

The Suffering Christ

Jesus entered the world stage during a time of great darkness. Roman conquerors ruled the Israelites with an iron fist and imposed such steep taxes on them that most families lived in deep poverty, forced into a vegetarian diet because they didn't have enough money to buy meat. Disease was rampant, and life expectancy was very short. At least half the children died before they could reach adulthood. Such poverty forced many into lives of crime, becoming thieves who lay in wait to attack travelers making their way along the isolated roads of the Judean countryside. It had been almost five hundred years since the last recorded prophet gave God's word to the suffering people, and they were crying out for the appearance of the promised Messiah.

11. Murray, "God Weeps."

Into this world, a child was born who was to be called Emmanuel, meaning "God with us." Through this child Jesus, God came and walked among us in human form, fully human and fully divine. Through Jesus, God experienced all of what it means to be human—the indignities, the suffering, the hunger and want. As one of us, Jesus grew up immersed in the social and political realities of the day, and his ministry demonstrates his deep identification with those who suffer. Jesus did not work his way up through the ranks to a position of power and leadership in the church, but chose to stand outside the walls of power and challenge the corruption and hypocrisy of the system. And in the process, Jesus himself suffered most grievously.

As I write this, it is Lent, and the calendar is marching on toward Holy Week and the story of Jesus' journey to the cross, seven days that encapsulate all that he stood for and how much he was willing to suffer for the sake of a suffering humanity. The abuse that Jesus endured during those final days can speak deeply to survivors of sexual abuse. Elaine Heath points out that Jesus himself was a victim of sexual abuse on that horrific Friday. She writes, "In Jesus' culture, as in Middle Eastern cultures today, to be stripped naked in front of a watching crowd was an act of sexual violation."[12] Stripped naked, whipped and beaten, spat upon by his tormentors and nailed to a cross, Jesus knew the shame of his nude body being used by others in a sickening and perverted display of power. Despite the strategically placed loin cloth depicted in religious art and on crucifixes, Jesus had no such protection from the humiliation of public display. Historians tell us that in biblical times, all condemned prisoners were, in fact, crucified naked. Indeed, Jesus knows firsthand the powerlessness of abuse victims at the hands of those who would use the bodies of innocents in their quest for the sick mixture of pleasure and power.

And because of Christ's anguished plea on the cross, we know that he felt abandoned and forsaken by God, a feeling that survivors know too well. But would God actually have abandoned God's beloved Son? "Would the Father really have looked away from his Son at the moment of Jesus' greatest saving act? This seems unthinkable. . . . (It is) more likely that God never removed his gaze from Jesus during those hours on the cross."[13] Instead, Adam Hamilton suggests that Jesus' cry arose from his utterly human doubt and despair. In the midst of the pain and loneliness of his suffering,

12. Heath, *The Least of These*, 123.
13. Hamilton, *24 Hours*, 108.

126

God, the Father, felt so very far away, and hope seemed out of reach. Perhaps it is the mark of suffering that in our darkest hours, our pain becomes a barrier to our ability to sense God's presence, even though God is most assuredly still with us, weeping over us, and sharing in our suffering. Maybe survivors can take comfort in the idea that Jesus, too, knows what it means to feel the emptiness of believing that God had turned away from him in his hour of greatest need. Perhaps the events of Good Friday will also allow them to experience the hope that, just as God did not abandon Jesus, God has never truly abandoned any of God's suffering children.

When we look at Jesus' final days, the extent of the pain and suffering that he endured, it is sometimes difficult to stomach the theory of atonement that proclaims that Jesus died as a substitute or sacrifice for the forgiveness of our sins. It makes us wonder what kind of God would demand the death of a scapegoat in order to make forgiveness possible, especially since, through the prophets, God had declared time after time that God despised the sacrificial system. God repeatedly expressed to the Israelites how much God longed for them to return to right relationship through repentance and a pure heart. What many don't realize is that there are other theories, some of them centuries old and widely accepted by the church, which put a different spin on the atonement altogether.

There is a growing body of theological thought that proposes that the whole point of the cross was Jesus' absolute solidarity with human suffering. Joseph Campbell states, "Jesus' death on the cross was not as ransom paid, or as penalty applied, but an act of atonement, at-one-ment, with the human race."[14] In other words, Jesus came to be "at one" with humanity, to finally and for all time bridge the gap between God and humankind. Walter Wink expands on Campbell when he says, "As the Crucified, Jesus thus identifies with every victim of torture, incest, or rape. . . . In Jesus we see the suffering of God *with and in* suffering people" (emphasis mine).[15] By experiencing all that human life contains—the blood, sweat, and tears, the joys and sorrows of human relationship, the hunger, homelessness, and hopelessness, even the betrayal, abandonment, abuse, and death—Jesus effectively erased the chasm that was fixed between human and divine in the garden of Eden.

Mark's gospel tells us that when Jesus gave up his last breath on the cross, the veil in the temple was torn in two (Mark 15:38). This veil was a

14. Campbell, cited in Linn et al., *Good Goats,* 58.
15. Wink, cited in Thornton, *Broken Yet Beloved,* 14.

curtain that separated the people worshiping in the temple from the holy of holies, the mysterious place where it was believed that God resided. With Jesus' death on the cross, this veil was no longer a barrier to human access to God. God was no longer contained by temple walls and curtains, but was turned loose to live in human hearts, to be accessible to all who call upon God's name, and to be a compassionate presence with all who suffer. Jesus provided the means by which all can experience union with God, no matter who they are or what they have experienced. Through Christ, we are able to partake in the new covenant, a covenant of forgiveness, grace, and compassion for all who turn to God.

HEALING PRACTICE 2

While Catholics often wear crucifixes as a reminder of Christ's sacrifice for us, Protestants have long rejected the crucifix in favor of the empty cross, which emphasizes the Resurrection. Unfortunately, removing Christ from the cross has sanitized it and distanced us from the experience of his suffering. It removes us from the conditions in which Jesus lived, as well as the blood, sweat, and tears of his death on the cross.

- Consider buying a crucifix, either as a necklace to wear or a statue to hang on your wall or place on a surface where you will see it regularly. As you wear or gaze at this crucifix, reflect on the suffering Christ and what this says about his great compassion for all who suffer.

- Imagine that this Jesus, who experienced the agony of physical and sexual abuse and the rending of his body on the cross, is looking into your eyes and feeling your pain. Allow yourself to receive this look of compassion and love.

Here, There, and Everywhere

There is an interesting dichotomy that happens with sexual abuse survivors. Because children have no other point of reference, and because abusers frequently portray their actions as a game or something they are compelled to do, young victims often make the assumption that the abuse is normal, that it's happening to everyone. If, for example, it is their grandfather who is abusing them, they believe that other children are also being molested by their grandfathers. But when, as they get older, they discover that this is not the case, they suddenly feel all alone in the world. Their shame tends to cause them to isolate from others, so they rarely share their abuse stories and therefore don't get to know other survivors. From inside this bubble, they look out at a world in which other people look happy and confident and fulfilled. Their isolation prevents them from seeing that, in one way or another, everyone suffers. Instead, they may come to believe that they alone have been singled out for such pain and anguish, which then intensifies their suffering.

The truth is that suffering is universal. Everyone suffers. While my suffering may not look the same as your suffering, the *experience* of suffering is still a unifying thread among all human beings. It is common for abuse survivors to compare what they have suffered with the pain of others, but in the process they either minimize their own brokenness or deny the suffering of the other, thus further isolating themselves from someone who could offer compassion and understanding.

Buddhism teaches that suffering is part of life, yet in the materialistic and prosperity-focused world of today, many seem to expect a life *without* suffering. Yancey states, "We moderns have cut ourselves off from the stream of human history, which has always accepted pain as an integral part of life."[16] Sadly, this expectation actually *increases* our suffering. And would we really want a world in which suffering does not exist? What would that world look like? There have been many utopian movies made over the years in which what first looked like utopia ultimately turned into a completely programmed world in which choice was lost. Individuality, emotion, and freedom were sacrificed for the sake of bland sameness and meaningless relationships. But often in these movies, a spark of humanity remained and was fanned into a rebellion against this gray, monotonous, and unfeeling world. And in the process of carrying out this revolt, people suffered—willingly.

It is human nature to have an aversion to pain. Most of us try to avoid it if we can. However, our capacity to experience joy is directly proportional to our willingness to accept sorrow in our lives. Many centuries ago, St. Augustine recognized this truth when he said, "Everywhere a greater joy is preceded by a greater suffering."[17] And in the early 1900s, Kahlil Gibran, a Lebanese-American poet and philosopher, wrote poignantly:

16. Yancey, *Where Is God*, 47.
17. Ibid., 53.

. . . the selfsame well from which your laughter rises was often-times filled with your tears. And how else can it be? The deeper that sorrow carves into your being, the more joy you can contain. Is not the cup that holds your wine the cup that was burned in the potter's oven? And is not the lute that soothes your spirit the very wood that was hollowed with knives?[18]

And what does it mean to accept the suffering in our lives, to recognize that suffering is part and parcel of what it means to be human? It seems to me that when we stop railing at God about what has happened to us, when we stop asking why or shaking our fists at the unfairness of it all, a great deal of energy is suddenly available for the task of healing. Survivors find themselves suddenly able to move forward, to look around and notice the blessings that are present in their lives. They are able to stop viewing themselves as victims and claim the label of survivor, recognizing the strength and courage it took for them to get to this point in their journey toward healing.

However, it is important not to mistake acceptance for resignation. Survivors of abuse do not have to be resigned to their suffering. This makes them vulnerable to further victimization. Jesus did not teach his followers to just take whatever abuses were handed to them. Instead, he fought against the powers that be, challenged the status quo, and sought to bring hope to the suffering masses. Jesus brought healing to all who sought him and challenged them to live in ways that brought healing to the world. This is the challenge today, not only for survivors of child sexual abuse, but for all whose lives are touched by this horrendous violation of the bodies and souls of our children. To paraphrase Philip Yancey, we have not only the right but the deep obligation to fight against the social, psychological, and political conditions that continue to cause suffering in our world.[19] I believe that it is in this fight that survivors can find wholeness and meaning.

HEALING PRACTICE 3

There is an ancient Chinese legend of a woman whose son had died. Her grief was so deep that she was unable to do anything but cry out in her sorrow day and night. After many weeks of overwhelming grief, her husband urged her to go to the holy man who lived in their village and ask his advice. At first, she refused to go,

18. Gibran, The Prophet, 32.
19. Yancey, Where Is God, 98.

but finally she plodded down the dusty road to the hut of the great teacher. "Teacher," she said, "What can I do to relieve this pain that sits like a stone on my heart?" The wise man answered, "Fetch me a mustard seed from a home that has never known sorrow. We will use it to drive the sorrow out of your life."[20] Begrudgingly, because she was tired and stiff from all of her sitting and sorrowing, the woman began her journey from door to door throughout the village seeking the mustard seed. For many days, she entered the homes of her neighbors and asked them if they had experienced suffering. Eventually, she returned to the abode of the teacher. The holy man noticed that her step seemed lighter and her face was no longer cast in the deep lines of grief. "And what did you find, my daughter?" he asked. The woman smiled, a very hint of a smile to be sure, but a smile nonetheless. "I did not find a mustard seed, Master, but something greater—compassion. I have discovered that all people suffer. I have spent these days sharing stories and tears and being touched by the courage of my neighbors in the face of many trials. Who am I to spend my days locked up within my own soul, when so many are in need of a word of comfort and love?" And thus she went on her way, spending her remaining days in loving service to all who came to her for solace.

- What does this story mean to you? In what ways does it speak to your own experience?

- By comforting and ministering to others, have you found relief from your own suffering?

- How does the understanding that suffering is a universal part of life make a difference to your own woundedness? What might you do to emulate the woman in the story?

HEALING PRACTICE 4

As you have read this book, and especially this chapter, your suffering is probably coming into sharper focus. It is likely that you have been remembering the pain of your childhood sexual abuse. You also may already have achieved some level of healing.

- Rituals of healing or letting go can be very powerful for survivors. Try creating a ritual that helps you remember and honor your suffering at the same time as you resolve to put it behind you and move forward into a hopeful future.

20. Ibid., 197.

- Offer your suffering to God as reflected in the following haiku:

Receive my sorrow,

Become the sacred bowl that

Holds my offering.

- Other examples of healing rituals may include lighting a candle in remembrance of the abused child you once were, burning something that represents the abuse for you, or performing some sort of cleansing ritual in which you wash away all of your old, negative beliefs about yourself as deserving of abuse, replacing them with a new identity as a beloved child of God, holy, whole, and undefiled.

10

"Where Can I Get This Living Water?"

Finding Hope, Transformation, and Meaning

"Jesus replied, 'People soon become thirsty again after drinking this water.
But the water I give them takes away thirst altogether. It becomes a
perpetual spring within them, giving them eternal life.'"
—JOHN 4:13–14 (NLT)

Hope

I want to begin our discussion on hope by revisiting the story of Jesus'
encounter with the woman at the well (John 4:1–30), first discussed in
chapter 5. Jesus and the disciples have been walking along dry, dusty roads
for many miles. It is midday, and they are tired and hungry. Jesus sends
the disciples into town to find food while he waits at the well. A Samaritan
woman is there drawing water, even though it is customary for women to
get their water in the cool morning hours. Jesus might have wondered why
she was there in the middle of the day, but he is thirsty and has no bucket,
so he asks this woman if she will give him something to drink. She is caught
off guard by Jesus' approach, for Jews believed that Samaritans were unclean
and would not speak to them, much less drink something that a Samaritan
had touched. When she calls him out on his impropriety, he responds with
a mysterious comment about living water. Since well water is usually just
stagnant rain water, the woman immediately wants to know where such liv-

ing water can be found. Her question is dripping with disbelief. Who does this stranger think he is—some kind of miracle worker?

The conversation becomes even more bizarre when Jesus tells her that this magic water quenches thirst permanently and gives the one who partakes of it eternal life. Still skeptical, the woman nevertheless doesn't want to miss out on a good thing and asks again for this water of which he speaks. Ah, but there's a catch! "Go and bring your husband here," he says. Immediately, the woman knows she is doomed, for she is living in sin with a man who is not her husband. This and her five previous marriages are the reason she comes to the well alone, to avoid the contemptuous remarks and sneering glances from the other women of the village. Reluctant and ashamed, she confesses that she is not married, but Jesus seems to already know her life story. And he doesn't care! He continues their conversation despite her shameful status, speaking to her about God and the nature of true worship. And when she states her belief in the coming Messiah, he tells her that he is the one! The promised Savior is speaking to her about a place in the kingdom!

This passage is one of great hope for survivors of child sexual abuse. Here is a story about a woman who could have been one of them! Given what we know about the long-term effects of abuse—promiscuity and un-healthy relationships—it isn't much of a stretch to infer that a woman who had lived with six different men had been a victim of some kind of sexual violation. Survivors can relate to her isolation and shame. And then to real-ize that despite the life she was leading, Jesus offered her living water and revealed himself as the Messiah feels like a stunning act of grace. To be blessed when one expects to be cursed, this is a moment of joy gushing forth like the clean and flowing water of which Jesus speaks. And so we begin our discussion of the hope, transformation, and meaning that is pos-sible to attain on this journey toward healing.

The last we hear of the Samaritan woman is that she went back to her village to tell the people about her encounter with Jesus and to wonder aloud, "Could this be the Christ?" (John 4:29) We don't know what hap-pened after that or how she was changed by the presence of the living God, but my guess is that a seed was planted in her soul that day, giving her the strength, hope, and courage to heal from the wounds of her abuse and be-gin a new life. Another sexual abuse survivor who can testify to the power of a seed is Paul Young, author of *The Shack*. In an article in *Guideposts*, Young shares his story of abuse, adultery, loss, and redemption. After his wife discovered his infidelity, Young was forced to face his abuse and all that it had cost him. Despairing, angry, and suicidal, he relates a day when he was so overcome by these feelings that he went to an old barn and began to hurl rotten apples, watching them explode against the walls of the barn. Looking at the pulpy mess he had made on the ground and sensing that the apples were an apt metaphor for his life, he bent over and picked up a solitary apple seed. How did this seed fit into the picture, he wondered? And somehow he knew the answer even in his present darkness: a seed could *grow*. [1]

In fact, we know that seeds begin their life in darkness. Much of their growth happens hidden in the earth before we ever see tender shoots springing forth. The psalmist echoes this hope in the seeds described in Psalm 126:

> When the Divine Lover enters the
> > human heart,
> > > all yearnings are fulfilled!
> Then will our mouths ring forth
> > > with laughter, and
> > > our tongues with shouts of joy;
> Then will we sing our songs of praise,
> > to You, O Beloved of all hearts.
> For gladness will radiate out for
> > all to see;
> > so great is your Presence
> > > among us.
> Restore us to wholeness, O Healer,
> > like newborn babes who have
> > > never strayed from You!
> May all who sow in tears
> > reap with shouts of joy!
> May all who go forth weeping tears
> > of repentance,
> > bearing seed for sowing,
> Come home to You with shouts
> > Of joy,
> > > leaving sorrow behind. [2]

1. Young, "The Healing," 78.
2. Merrill, *Psalms for Praying*, 274.

HEALING PRACTICE 1

The Samaritan woman was in a state of brokenness when she encountered Jesus at the well. You may identify with her shame, suspicion, and fear as part of your own aftermath of abuse. Imagine what it might have felt like to be in the divine presence and feel the acceptance and love he gave so freely. Imagine the sensation of a shower of the living water that Christ offers flowing over you. Remember a time when you were hot and thirsty and you were able to drink deeply from a cup of pure, cool water. This is what it might feel like to receive the living waters of healing and redemption that Christ offers to all. Feel the hope that arises in you as you pray with this excerpt from Psalm 7:

Arise, O Beloved, in your steadfast love,
    shield me from the demons within;
Stay near me, Heart of my heart, and
    I shall be strong to face
        my fears.
Let all the fragmented parts of my being
    gather around You,
    help me to face them one by one.
Love's healing presence will mend
    all that has been broken,
    and I shall be made whole.[3]

Without doubt, our best example of hope bursting forth from darkness is in the resurrection of Jesus Christ. In the previous chapter, we dealt with Jesus' suffering on the cross and, through that act, his solidarity with all human suffering. But the story doesn't end there! All hope for the coming kingdom of God rests on the resurrection. Death is not the end; it is the act of rising from the tomb that completes the pattern of suffering and redemption. And it is the circumstances of Jesus' death that point the way to our hope in the kingdom. Jesus died to show us a different way, to reveal a kingdom in which there is a great reversal of power, where military might and violence do not rule, where money and selfish ambition are not the prerequisites for sitting in the seats of power. The whole reason that Jewish and Roman leaders wanted Jesus dead is that all his teachings were about turning the prevailing power structure on its head! Jesus taught that the

3. Ibid., 9.

last shall be first (Matt 19:30), the one who humbles himself will be exalted (Luke 14:11), and the kingdom of heaven belongs to those who are poor in spirit. (Matt 5:3)

This kind of kingdom speaks volumes to survivors of sexual abuse who have suffered the worst cruelty that powerful and violent offenders can perpetrate on another human being. Jesus, through his ministry, dying, and rising, leads the way to a world where love, selfless service, and nonviolence hold sway over vice, violence, and corruption. It is a world that is in some ways both already here among us and also not yet. Every time someone offers kindness to a stranger or refuses to tolerate hatred and violence or takes a stand against corrupt systems of power, the kingdom of God is here now. Every time love triumphs over hate, everywhere that children are protected from the depredations of sexual predators, every moment in which there is a glimmer of hope and healing, the reign of Heaven becomes a reality. But we all long for a day when the kingdom comes in fullness and no one has to suffer anymore. This is the day Isaiah speaks of when he says:

> Behold, I will create new heavens and a new earth. The former things will not be remembered, nor will they come to mind. . . . I will rejoice over Jerusalem and take delight in my people; the sound of weeping and of crying will be heard in it no more. Never again will there be in it an infant who lives but a few days, or an old man who does not live out his years . . . . (Isa 65:17–20a)

In this new world,

> the wolf will live with the lamb, the leopard will lie down with the goat, the calf and the lion and the yearling together; and a little child will lead them . . . . The infant will play near the hole of the cobra, and the young child put his hand into the viper's nest. They will neither harm nor destroy on all my holy mountain . . . . (Isa 11:6, 8–9a)

HEALING PRACTICE 2

Read 2 Corinthians 4:8–10. When you look at your suffering as deeply connected to the suffering, death, and resurrection of Christ, does it give you hope for your own "resurrection"?

- Consider the possibility that you can become a living testament to God's power to bring life from death, hope from despair, and healing from brokenness.

- Are there ways in which you are already this kind of witness to others?

- Allow the divine gardener to plant a seed of hope in your soul that even more healing will come.

Another example of this concept of both now and not yet is found in the central narrative of Hebrew Scripture, the exodus. The exodus story, "a story of bondage, liberation, a journey, and a destination",[4] tells us of a captive people, kept as slaves for over 200 years. Certainly, survivors of sexual abuse will resonate with these people who cried out to God to rescue them from their bondage. Their skin scarred with the whips of their taskmasters, their backs bent by the loads they carried, their spirits crushed by their oppressors, women and children likely raped by their captors as a show of dominance and power, they mindlessly toiled through their days, bereft of hope and mired in despair. And yet the longed-for liberation finally did come. Just as for most survivors whose abuse eventually stopped; the captives were released from their oppressors in God's act of mercy through God's servant, Moses.

But liberation is only the beginning of the story. The word "exodus" means "the way out," and sometimes the way out is fraught with peril.[5] The journey unfolds as a people are led through the wilderness toward the Promised Land. Like the survivor's journey towards healing, it is a long and treacherous road with many dangers and setbacks to be faced. In the biblical Exodus story, the Israelites are frightened and unsure. Their lives have been dictated by their captors for as long as they can remember, and they have no idea how to be the masters of their own destiny. They encounter hunger, thirst, illness, isolation, and conflict, yet through it all, they are guided by the presence of God in the pillar of cloud by day and the pillar of fire by night. They learn to trust that God is with them through every trial. Marcus Borg tells us that their destination, the promised land, is life in the presence of God. "Yet God is not simply the destination, but one who is known on the journey. It is a journeying *toward* God that is also *with* God."[6]

I believe that many survivors go through their own exodus journey of bondage, liberation, journey, and destination. Their experience of child sexual abuse was one of bondage, of being held captive by the controlling

4. Borg, *Meeting Jesus*, 123.
5. Ibid.
6. Ibid., 125.

ways of their abusers, by their fear and shame, and by the secrecy through which their abuser was able to continue perpetrating such horrible acts. Then, whether through the offender's illness, death, or apprehension by authorities, life circumstances, fears of being caught, or the onset of a victim's adulthood, the abuse stops. Liberation! Then the journey begins, a journey toward healing that starts with an awareness of all that was lost. This may be the first time that an abuse survivor is able to truly experience all their feelings about what happened—the searing pain and grief, the raging anger, the overwhelming fear, the deep uncertainty about who they are and where to go from here. But as we have seen from our exploration of Christ's own suffering, we can be sure that God is there in the midst of this journey. Just as God made God's presence known to the Israelites through pillars of cloud and fire, God will also be made known in the healing journeys of abuse survivors. Survivors can have hope that their journey toward God is also a journey *with* God. They can have hope for the kingdom of heaven that is both now and not yet. The promised land is within us, a seed growing in the darkness, waiting for a time when it will burst forth in all its glory. The promised land is the home of living water, life with God.

Transformation

On a trip to Florida to visit my daughter several years ago, we had brunch at a restaurant she frequented. When I went into the bathroom to wash my hands, I was struck by the unique and lovely mosaic on the wall. Broken bits of pottery in many colors had been affixed to the wall in a beautiful pattern. When I asked my daughter about this, she said that when the restaurant was first opening, they had ordered custom coffee mugs with their logo on them. Unfortunately, when they arrived and the cases were opened, many of the mugs were broken. Of course, the manufacturer replaced them, but an artistic employee suggested that the broken pieces might be used to create a unique décor on their bathroom walls. It occurred to me that this was illustrative of the way in which brokenness can often be transformed into something beautiful. Julian of Norwich, a fourteenth-century Benedictine nun, believed that when the Great Physician heals our wounds, we become even more beautiful than if we'd never been broken.[7]

Perhaps we can think of God as a "found items" artist who reclaims people that others have abused, misused, broken, or discarded, and creates

7. Heath, *The Least of These*, 117.

something both exquisite and valuable with their lives. One of the sure markers that a survivor of child sexual abuse is making progress on their healing journey is when they begin to recognize the positive things that have come out of their abuse. They can even be grateful for some of the ways in which they were, by the grace of God, transformed by it. This is a crucial step, because, in the words of Richard Rohr, "If we do not transform our pain, we will most assuredly transmit it."[8] This is not to say that survivors should be grateful for the abuse, but just like victims of earthquakes or tornados who are sometimes able to find treasure in the midst of the rubble of their belongings, there are often gifts to be gleaned from the rubble of an abuse survivor's brokenness.

For example, during a session with Terri, I asked her if she could identify any of her positive traits as the transformative effects of her abuse. After thinking about this for a while, she responded, "Well, I have this big old heart." She understood that her deep compassion arose from having been deeply wounded herself and that her ability to empathize with others had value. She and another client, Nicole, were both teachers who had an instinctive understanding of the needs of their students who were struggling. Even though there were times when they were unable to change a student's circumstances, their compassion allowed them to be present to the child's pain, so that he or she felt heard and understood, something very precious and rare. Therefore, despite the times when their hearts were broken by a child who was obviously hurting, they wouldn't have chosen not to possess this gift.

Abuse survivors know firsthand what it means to be beaten and battered by life, to feel outside the circle of human connection—isolated, ashamed, and alone. As excruciating as that experience is, being on the outside looking in is exactly the vantage point from which one can see clearly the pain of the world and the systems that rule by climbing over the broken backs of their victims. Rohr says, "That place outside of the system is a 'liminal space' where transformation and conversion is much more likely."[9] For some, the abuse breaks down their ego, creating a servant mentality in which they can use their skills to help and serve others rather than to use others for their own ego needs. This does not mean that survivors should become subservient; rather, their abuse gives them a greater capacity for compassion, empathy, and identification with the pain of others and, along

8. Rohr, *Things Hidden*, 25.
9. Ibid., 104.

with these things, the power to reach out to people in helpful and healing ways.

Survivors also have a hard-won ability to see what is important in this world and what is not. They tend to see through the petty squabbles and distractions in which other people engage and focus on what is real and lasting. And often they are more able to notice and appreciate the small pleasures that others take for granted. Nicole's abusive father hated the Christmas holidays and refused to have a Christmas tree in the house. While the family did exchange small gifts, they were usually essentials such as new pajamas or underwear, and there was nothing festive about it. As an adult, Nicole bought herself an artificial tree which she kept up in her home year-round, decorating it with ornaments associated with whatever holiday was being celebrated in any given month. In February, the tree was festooned with hearts, and in July it sported red, white, and blue. This simple act of reclaiming the holidays for herself gave her great joy.

Other traits that often arise from the suffering of abuse survivors are strength, courage, perseverance, patience, and wisdom. When Terri was diagnosed with breast cancer, her friends were in awe of her strength and determination. She faced the cancer head on, researched the best treatment protocols, consulted with her doctors, and soldiered on through difficult and uncomfortable procedures. Of course, there were bad days when anger and fear overwhelmed her, but never did she indulge in self-pity. When I remarked on how well she was coping with this ordeal, her response was a matter-of-fact "What's the alternative?"

Wisdom and insight often come from having seen way more of the dark side of life than anyone ever should. Some survivors seem to understand human nature better than people who have never walked through the dark vale of sexual abuse. Perhaps Aeschylus, the father of ancient Greek tragedy, put it best: "Pain that cannot forget falls drop by drop upon the heart until in our despair there comes wisdom through the awful grace of God."[10]

I mentioned in chapter 4 that many survivors seem hungry for God, even though they struggle to understand God's part in their abuse. Richard Rohr states that suffering "carves out the space within us for deep desire."[11] Human pain and struggle create in us a longing for God as we cry out for love, comfort, and healing. For those rare people who have not experienced

10. Brainy Quote, "Aeschylus."
11. Rohr, *Things Hidden,* 180.

any kind of suffering, God may seem irrelevant. They are indifferent to God and feel no need of something more. But those who long for God are met and filled by God's longing for them. This is indeed a transforming gift born out of the ashes of abuse. In *Broken Yet Beloved*, Sharon Thornton writes, "God chooses to be where suffering is. God seeks to relieve suffering not necessarily through a direct and triumphant overcoming of suffering, but through the hidden transformation of suffering that can sometimes come as a surprise."[12]

HEALING PRACTICE 3

In *Everything Belongs*, Richard Rohr writes, "The path of prayer and love and the path of suffering seem to be the two Great Paths of transformation."[13] Take some time to think about how this applies to your life.

- Can you identify the positive ways in which you have been transformed by the abuse you suffered?

- In the economy of the kingdom, nothing is wasted. God is a creative God with the infinite capacity to transform the worst pain the world can inflict into something of beauty, value, and meaning. Have you begun to experience this yet? Can you acknowledge and receive this gift?

- See if you can find something that is torn or broken, whether it is one of your belongings or something you find at a thrift store. Try to find a new and beautiful use for this item. Some ideas might be to make a small quilt from pieces of fabric cut from old clothing or to press broken pieces of pottery into the shape of a cross in plaster of paris. Let your imagination guide you into creating something lovely from that which has been broken. Meditate on the ways God has done this in your life.

Meaning

One of the tasks that may be addressed in the later stages of a survivor's healing journey is that of seeking to find the meaning of the abuse, to make sense of it. Rather than viewing themselves as defined by the abuse,

12. Thornton, *Broken Yet Beloved*, 86.
13. Rohr, *Everything Belongs*, 14–15.

survivors seek to integrate their experience into the whole of who they are. In early stages, being an abuse survivor seems to be their entire identity, as if they were just one large, pulsing ball of pain. The pain is the only thing they know and the only viewpoint from which to see the world around them. With time and the help of a therapist, spiritual director, and/or loving relationships, the wound begins to shrink and heal, allowing more of the true self to emerge and grow. It is at this point that the possibility of discovering a meaning that transcends the abuse can open up. And it is when they are able to connect their own story to a larger story that the way forward is revealed. Richard Rohr writes:

> All of our (stories) take on a transcendent meaning when we can connect them to (Christ's) Story. Even our wounds become sacred wounds by reason of seeing them inside of this Big Picture. For Christians, we learn to identify our own wounds with the wounding of Jesus and the sufferings of the universal Body of Christ.[14]

And it is this awareness of a suffering humanity that calls all of us to action.

Leo Tolstoy once wrote, "It is by those who have suffered that the world has been advanced."[15] When our gaze moves from our deep inner pain outward to the suffering of the world, we are able to expand our outrage to include the people and systems that harm all of our fellow travelers in life. Tempered by compassion and channeled into action, this anger can transform abuse survivors into tireless workers in the fight against evil, injustice, and oppression in every form. In the words of Saint Augustine, "Hope has two lovely daughters. They are Anger and Courage. Anger that things are not what they ought to be, and Courage to see that they do not remain as they are."[16]

Having important work to do, work that benefits a wounded humanity, seems to be a vital part of the healing process.[17] Perhaps it is the survivor's true task not to discover the "why" of human suffering, but instead to identify and work to eradicate the conditions that cause and perpetuate it.[18] We live in an imperfect world. God's work of creation is not finished yet. Perhaps meaning can be found as we seek to co-create with God a world in which children are safe from abuses of all kinds, in which fear and pain are

14. Rohr, *Things Hidden*, 24.

15. Inspirational Quotes, Words, and Sayings, "Leo Tolstoy Quotes."

16. Goodreads, "Augustine of Hippo."

17. Thornton, *Broken Yet Beloved*, 197.

18. Ibid., 4.

only echoes from a remembered past and not an ever-present reality. And until that day comes, we must bear witness to the abuse of those who have no voice, remove the cloak of secrecy that hides child sexual abuse from the eyes of a willfully ignorant society, and advocate for all of its innocent victims.

It was Gandhi who taught us to become the change we wish to see in the world. We are all members of a common humanity, and the survival of the human family is dependent on the well-being of each of its members. God calls us to love and serve one another, to seek the lost, to heal the sick and wounded, and to console the brokenhearted. Jesus said, "I assure you, when you did (these things) to one of the least of these my brothers and sisters, you were doing it to me!" (Matt 25:40, NLT) Survivors know full well what it feels like to be "the least of these," yet healing and transformation offer hope that they can be empowered to become agents of change, allowing them to reach out to others who are in the same place of helplessness and hopelessness in which they themselves used to dwell. This empowerment comes from a God who loves and heals. Suffering can be a crucible in which a deeper connection with the Divine can be forged. And out of that transforming fire can rise a newness of life that reaches out and seeks to transform the world. Hope leads to transformation, transformation leads to meaning, and meaning leads to these triumphant words from Joseph to the brothers who had sold him into slavery: "You intended to harm me, but God intended it for good to accomplish what is now being done, the saving of many lives" (Gen 50:20).

HEALING PRACTICE 4

"Perhaps we cannot prevent this world from being a world in which children are tortured. But we can reduce the number of tortured children. And if you don't help us, who else in the world can help us do this."[19] As you reflect on these words from Albert Camus, be aware of the feelings that arise in you.

- Do they frighten you? That's OK. Very little that's worth doing in this world doesn't scare us.

- Do they energize you to join the battle? What can you do to forward the cause of reducing the number of sexually abused

19 Quotes, "Albert Camus."

children in the world today? Is there some way in which you are already making a difference?

- Consider the meaning that taking up this challenge would give to the abuse you have suffered. Remember that we are all members of the human family, and when one suffers we all suffer. Your path won't be easy, but it will be worth it in the end.

I'd like to close with these words from someone who has been there:

> It will be hard and people will try to knock you off the path you are on . . . and you'll feel so alone and you'll cry and your tears will fill a bucket and that bucket will become your wishing well and then if you pray that bucket will become your mirror and you'll see the face of God.[20]

---

20. Anonymous, cited in Thornton, *Broken Yet Beloved,* 214.

Bibliography

American Psychiatric Association. *Diagnostic and Statistical Manual of Mental Disorders,* 4th ed. Washington, DC: American Psychiatric Association, 1994.

Ashcroft, Mary Ellen. *Dogspell: A Dogmatic Theology on the Abounding Love of God.* Leavenworth, KS: Forest of Peace., 2000.

Barclay, William. Cited in Linn, et al. *Good Goats: Healing Our Image of God.* New York: Paulist, 1994.

Bell, Rob. *Love Wins: A Book About Heaven, Hell, and the Fate of Every Person Who Ever Lived.* New York: Harper One, 2011.

Bolen, Jean Shinoda. *Goddesses in Older Women: Archetypes in Women Over Fifty.* New York: Harper Perennial, 2001.

Berg, Amy, dir. *Deliver Us from Evil: Innocence and Faith Betrayed.* Disarming, 2006.

Borg, Marcus J. *The Heart of Christianity: Rediscovering a Life of Faith.* New York: HarperCollins, 2003.

———. *Meeting Jesus Again for the First Time: The Historical Jesus and the Heart of Contemporary Faith.* New York: HarperOne, 1994.

Boros, Ladislaus. "Regarding the Theology of Death." In *Readings in Christian Eschatology,* 124–143, edited by Franz Mussner. Derby, NY: Society of St. Paul, 1966.

Brainy Quote. "Aeschylus." http://www.brainyquote.com/quotes/authors/a/aeschylus.html.

Carnes, Patrick. *The Betrayal Bond: Breaking Free of Exploitive Relationships.* Deerfield Beach, FL: Health Communications, 1997.

Carrol, Eamon R. "Marian Spirituality." In *Spiritual Traditions for the Contemporary Church,* edited by Robin Maas and Gabriel O'Donnell, 365–379. Nashville, TN: Abingdon, 1990.

Chandy, J. M., et al. "Female Adolescents with a History of Sexual Abuse: Risk, Outcomes and Protective Factors." *Journal of Interpersonal Violence* 11 (1996) 503–518.

Clark, Jerusha, with Earl Henslin. *Inside the Cutter's Mind: Understanding and Helping Those Who Self-Injure.* Colorado Springs, CO: NavPress THINK, 2007.

Courtois, Christine A. *Healing the Incest Wound: Adult Survivors in Therapy.* New York: W. W. Norton, 1988.

Cutajar, M., et al. "Suicide and fatal drug overdose in child sexual abuse victims: a historical cohort study." *Medical Journal of Australia* 192:4 (2010) 184–187.

Davis, Laura. *Allies in Healing: When the Person You Love Was Sexually Abused as a Child.* New York: HarperPerennial, 1991.

Deak, Esteban. *Apokatastasis: The Problem of Universal Salvation in Twentieth Century Theology.* Toronto: Esteban Deak, 1979.

DeLong, Amy E. "Clergy Covenant: An Invitation." https://www.yumpu.com/en/document/view/11255518/clergy-covenant-an-invitation-love-on-trial/3.

Driskell, Joseph D. "Spiritual Direction with Traumatized Persons." In *Still Listening: New Horizons in Spiritual Direction,* edited by Norvene Vest, 17–35. Harrisburg, PA: Morehouse, 2000.

Finkelhor, D., et al. "Sexual abuse and its relationship to later sexual satisfaction, marital status, religion and attitudes." *Journal of Interpersonal Violence* 4 (1989) 379–399.

Fowler, James W. *Stages of Faith: The Psychology of Human Development and the Quest for Meaning.* New York: HarperOne, 1981.

Freidman, S. R., and R. D. Enright. "Forgiveness as an intervention goal with incest survivors." *Journal of Consulting and Clinical Psychology* 64 (1996) 983–992.

Gibran, Kahlil. *The Prophet.* New York: Alfred A. Knopf, 1971.

Goodreads. "Augustine of Hippo." http://www.goodreads.com/quotes/107417.

Grand, Le. *The Puppy Who Chased the Sun.* New York: Wonder, 1950.

Guenther, Margaret. *Holy Listening: The Art of Spiritual Direction.* Cambridge, MA: Cowley, 1992.

Hafiz. "Stay With Us." In *The Gift: Poems by Hafiz, the Great Sufi Master,* translated by Daniel Ladinsky, 284–85. New York: Penguin Compass, 1999.

Hamilton, Adam. *24 Hours That Changed the World.* Nashville, TN: Abingdon, 2009.

Heath, Elaine. *We Were The Least of These: Reading the Bible with Survivors of Sexual Abuse.* Grand Rapids, MI: Brazos, 2011.

Herman, Judith Lewis. *Trauma and Recovery: The Aftermath of Violence—From domestic Abuse to Political Terror.* New York: HarperCollins, 1992.

Hope, Glenda B. "Bearing Witness to the Reign of God in the World." Presented at the Academy for Spiritual Formation, Burlingame, California, August 19–24, 2007.

Inspirational Quotes, Words, and Sayings. "Leo Tolstoy Quotes." http://www.inspirationslstories.com/quotes/.

Job, Rueben P., and Norman Shawchuck. *A Guide to Prayer for All Who Seek God.* Nashville, TN: Upper Room, 2003.

———. *A Guide to Prayer for All God's People.* Nashville, TN: Upper Room, 1990.

Linn, Dennis, et al. *Don't Forgive Too Soon: Extending the Two Hands That Heal.* New York: Paulist, 1997.

———. *Good Goats: Healing Our Image of God.* New York: Paulist, 1994.

———. *Understanding Difficult Scriptures in a Healing Way.* New York: Paulist, 2001.

McLaughlin, Barbara R. "Devastated Spirituality: The Impact of Clergy Sexual Abuse on the Survivor's Relationship with God and the Church." *Sexual Addiction and Compulsivity* 1 (1994) 145–158.

Merriam-Webster Dictionary. Springfield, MA: Merriam-Webster, 1997.

Merrill, Nan. *Psalms for Praying: An Invitation to Wholeness.* New York: Continuum, 1996.

Merton, Thomas. "Cables to the Ace." In *The Collected Poems of Thomas Merton,* 400. New York: New Directions, 1977.

Meyer, Rick. *Through the Fire: Spiritual Restoration for Adult Victims of Childhood Sexual Abuse.* Minneapolis, MN: Augsberg, 2005.

Mollenkott, Virginia Ramey. *The Divine Feminine: The Biblical Imagery of God as Female.* New York: Crossroad, 1994.

Moore, Christopher. *Lamb: The Gospel According to Biff, Christ's Childhood Pal.* New York: Harper Perennial, 2002.

Murray, Shirley Erena. Lyrics to "God Weeps." Carol Stream, IL: Hope, 1996.

Norris, Kathleen. *Amazing Grace: A Vocabulary of Faith.* New York: Riverhead, 1998.

Nouwen, Henri. *Behold the Beauty of the Lord: Praying with Icons.* Notre Dame, IN: Ave Maria, 1987.

Quotes. "Albert Camus." http://www.quotes.net/quote/52499.

Reiland, Rachel. *I'm Not Supposed to Be Here: My Recovery from Borderline Personality Disorder.* Milwaukee, WI: Eggshells, 2002.

Rilke, Rainer Maria. "Wir dürfen dich nicht eigenmachtig mälen." In *Rilke's Book of Hours: Love Poems to God,* translated by Anita Barrows and Joanna Macy, 50. New York: Riverhead, 1996.

Rohr, Richard. *Everything Belongs: The Gift of Contemplative Prayer.* New York: Crossroad, 2003.

———. *Things Hidden: Scripture as Spirituality.* Cincinnati, OH: St. Anthony Messenger, 2007.

Rubenstein, Richard L. *After Auschwitz: Radical Theology and Contemporary Judaism.* Indianapolis, IN/New York: Bobbs–Merrill, 1966.

Sanatan Society. "Hindu Gods and Goddesses." http://www.sanatansociety.org/hindu_gods_and_goddesses.htm#.VVKQC_y6eRo.

Scharf, Margaret. "Stages of Faith: Stages of Life." Presented at The Source at the Center I, Orange, CA, August 7, 2008.

Smedes, Lewis. *Forgive and Forget: Healing the Hurts We Don't Deserve.* San Francisco: HarperSanFrancisco, 1984.

Thangaraj, M. Thomas. "Christian Spirituality in the Global Context." Presented at the Academy for Spiritual Formation, Burlingame, CA, April 23–28, 2007.

Thornton, Susan G. *Broken Yet Beloved: A Pastoral Theology of the Cross.* St. Louis, MO: Chalice, 2002.

Van Wormer, Katherine, and Lois Berns. "The Impact of Priest Sexual Abuse: Female Survivors' Narratives." *Affilia* 19 (2004), 53–67."

Webster's New World Dictionary. 2nd college ed. New York: The World, 1970.

Wikipedia. "Repentance." http://en.wikipedia.org/wiki/Repentance.

Wink, Walter. *Engaging the Powers.* Minneapolis, MN: Fortress, 1992.

Wuellner, Flora Slosson. *Forgiveness, the Passionate Journey: Nine Steps of Forgiving Through Jesus' Beatitudes.* Nashville, TN: Upper Room, 2001.

Yaconelli, Michael. *Messy Spirituality.* Grand Rapids, MN: Zondervan, 2002.

Yancey, Philip. *Where is God When It Hurts.* Grand Rapids, MI: Zondervan, 1990.

Young, Paul. "The Healing." In *Guideposts* August (2009) 74–78.

———. *The Shack: Where Tragedy Confronts Eternity.* Los Angeles: Windblown Media, 2007.

APPENDIX A

Symptoms of Post-Traumatic Stress Disorder

(Adapted from the Diagnostic and Statistical Manual of Mental Disorders IV[1])

Criterion A: Stressor

The person was exposed to: death, threatened death, actual or threatened serious injury, or actual or threatened sexual violence.

Criterion B: Intrusive symptoms

The traumatic event is persistently re-experienced in at least one of the following ways:

1. Recurrent, involuntary, and intrusive memories.
2. Traumatic nightmares.
3. Dissociative reactions (e.g., flashbacks) which may occur on a continuum from brief episodes to complete loss of consciousness.
4. Intense or prolonged distress after exposure to traumatic reminders.
5. Significant bodily reactions after exposure to trauma-related stimuli.

Criterion C: Avoidance

Persistent and purposeful avoidance of distressing trauma-related stimuli, including one or both of the following:

1. American Psychiatric Association, *Diagnostic and Statistical Manual IV*, 427–429.

1. Trauma-related thoughts or feelings.

2. Trauma-related external reminders (e.g., people, places, objects, or situations).

Criterion D: Negative changes in thoughts and mood

Two or more negative changes in thought and/or mood that began or worsened after the traumatic event, such as:

1. Inability to recall key features of the traumatic event not due to head injury, alcohol, or drugs.

2. Persistent (and often distorted) negative beliefs and expectations about oneself or the world (e.g., "I am bad," "The world is completely dangerous.").

3. Persistent distorted blame of self or others for causing the traumatic event or for resulting consequences.

4. Persistent negative trauma-related emotions (e.g., fear, horror, anger, guilt, or shame).

5. Markedly diminished interest in (pre-trauma) significant activities.

6. Feeling alienated from others (e.g., detachment or estrangement).

7. Constricted affect; persistent inability to experience positive emotions.

Criterion E: Alterations in arousal and reactivity

Two or more trauma-related alterations in arousal and reactivity that began or worsened after the traumatic event:

1. Irritable or aggressive behavior.

2. Self-destructive or reckless behavior.

3. Hypervigilance, a sense of being constantly on guard, alert to potential danger.

4. Exaggerated startle response.

5. Problems in concentration.

6. Sleep disturbance.

The above symptoms persist for more than one month and create significant distress or impairment in social and/or occupational functioning.

APPENDIX B

Recommended Reading

On Sexual Abuse

The Betrayal Bond: Breaking Free of Exploitive Relationships. Patrick J. Carnes, PhD. Deerfield Beach, FL: Health Communications, 1997.

Courage to Heal: A Guide for Women Survivors of Child Sexual Abuse (4th ed.). Ellen Bass & Laura Davis. New York: William Morrow Paperbacks, 2008.

Through the Fire: Spiritual Restoration for Adult Victims of Childhood Sexual Abuse. Rick Meyer. Minneapolis: Augsburg, 2005.

The Wounded Heart: Hope for Adult Victims of Childhood Sexual Abuse. Dan B. Allender. Colorado Springs, CO: NavPress, 2008.

On Anger

Transforming Fire: Women Using Anger Creatively. Kathleen Fischer. New York: Paulist, 1999.

On Shame

Shame and Grace: Healing the Shame We Don't Deserve. Lewis Smedes. San Francisco: HarperSanFrancisco/Zondervan, 1993.

On Suffering

Disappointment with God: Three Questions No One Asks Aloud. Philip Yancey. Grand Rapids, MI: Zondervan, 1988.

The Shack: Where Tragedy Confronts Eternity. William P. Young. Los Angeles: Windblown, 2007.

When Bad Things Happen to Good People. Harold S. Kushner. New York: Anchor, 1981.
Where is God When it Hurts? Philip Yancey. Grand Rapids, MI: Zondervan, 1990.

On Forgiveness

Don't Forgive Too Soon: Extending the Two Hands That Heal. Dennis Linn, Sheila Fabricant Linn, & Matthew Linn. New York: Paulist, 1997.
Forgive and Forget: Healing the Hurts We Don't Deserve. Lewis Smedes. San Francisco: HarperSanFrancisco, 1984.
Forgiveness: The Passionate Journey. Flora Slosson Wuellner. Nashville: Upper Room, 2001.

On Sin, Heaven, and Hell

Good Goats: Healing Our Image of God. Dennis Linn, Sheila Fabricant Linn, & Matthew Linn. New York: Paulist, 1994.
The Heart of Christianity: Rediscovering a Life of Faith. Marcus J. Borg. New York: HarperOne, 1989.
Love Wins: A Book About Heaven, Hell, and the Fate of Every Person Who Ever Lived. Rob Bell. New York: HarperOne, 2011.

On the Bible

Soul Sisters: Women in Scripture Speak to Women Today. Edwina Gately. Maryknoll, NY: Orbis, 2002.
Things Hidden: Scripture as Spirituality. Richard Rohr. Cincinnati, OH: St. Anthony Messenger, 2008.
Understanding Difficult Scriptures in a Healing Way. Matthew Linn, Sheila Fabricant Linn, & Dennis Linn. New York: Paulist, 2001.
We Were the Least of These: Reading the Bible with Survivors of Sexual Abuse. Elaine Heath. Grand Rapids, MI: Brazos, 2011.

On Spirituality

An Altar in the World: A Geography of Faith. Barbara Brown Taylor. New York: HarperOne, 2009.
Everything Belongs: The Gift of Contemplative Prayer. Richard Rohr. New York: Crossroad, 1999.
Messy Spirituality. Michael Yaconelli. Grand Rapids, MI: Zondervan, 2002.

For Family and Friends

Allies in Healing: When the Person You Love Was Sexually Abused as a Child. Laura Davis.
New York: Harper Perennial, 1991.

For Spiritual Directors

Allies in Healing: When the Person You Love Was Sexually Abused as a Child. Laura Davis.
New York: Harper Perennial, 1991.
"Compassion for the Wounded Soul: Addressing Child Sexual Abuse in Spiritual
Direction." Sue Magrath, in *Presence: An International Journal of Spiritual Direction,*
19:2, June 2013.
"Spiritual Direction with Traumatized Persons," Joseph D. Driskill in *Still Listening:
NewHorizons in Spiritual Direction,* Norvene Vest, ed. Harrisburg, PA: Morehouse
Publishing, 2000.
Stages of Faith: The Psychology of Human Development and the Quest for Meaning. James
W. Fowler. New York: HarperOne, 1981.
*Trauma and Recovery: The Aftermath of Violence—From Domestic Abuse to Political
Terror.* Judith Lewis Herman, MD. New York: Basic, 1992.
Understanding Difficult Scriptures in a Healing Way. Matthew Linn, Sheila Fabricant Linn,
& Dennis Linn. New York: Paulist, 2001.
We Were the Least of These: Reading the Bible with Survivors of Sexual Abuse. Elaine Heath.
Grand Rapids, MI: Brazos, 2011.

With around 150 pages, this small book is rich in content.